PRAISE FOR

T0031902

"*Otters Dance* is a treatise _____ - life, family, and most of all a unique appreciation of our home state of Wyoming. The essays in this collection come from a lifetime of observing, listening to, and studying the land and the old-timers who were here before us. This is an absolute must-read for anyone who wants to understand the landscape, history, and culture of the rural Mountain West."

—**C. J. Box**, #1 *New York Times* Best-Selling Author
of *Shadows Reel*

"This is a book of wonders, revealing the enchantment of the natural world through the eyes of the keenest of observers. It is a book of science, explaining the interrelationship of humans, animals, habitat, and natural cycles with accessible and indelible clarity. Most of all, it is a book of hope, providing concrete examples of the ways that culture and the environment can heal through communication, collaboration, and mutual respect. I know of no more experienced or eloquent voice in the American West for the radical center, that ground on which human resiliency and healthy ecosystems meet. Bob Budd has devoted his life to building bridges between worlds that are often portrayed at odds: fifteen years as executive director of the Wyoming Stockgrowers, more than a decade managing the Red Canyon Ranch and serving as director of land management for The Nature Conservancy in Wyoming, and currently serving as executive director of the Wyoming Wildlife and Natural Resource Trust. This is a life-changing, even a world-saving book. Read it."

—**Teresa Jordan**, Author of
Riding the White Horse Home and
The Year of Living Virtuously (Weekends Off)

"Reading *Otters Dance* brought me right back to my roots and reminded me of how essential family and community are to each of us. *Otters Dance* rejuvenates the optimism that we can persevere with humility, grace, and a good deal of humor through difficult times. Growing up in Wyoming is special. I know nowhere else where you can meet a stranger, start a conversation, and in just a few minutes, know you know the same people. Bob's journey, his observations, and his delight at witnessing the partnership he has with nature bear fruit is the stuff us kids were fascinated to listen to when the early ranchers talked about their times. Those old-timers knew things about the music of the seasons, the poetry of life, and the wonder of it all, which we have lost. Bob's book brings back the perspective that we have lost as we focus too much on technology and precision modeling. Life is empirical by its very nature. Bob Budd tells us why it's important to be present in it."

—**Mark Gordon**, Governor of Wyoming

"Bob Budd's work is both introspective and as open as the land and people he deeply loves. He blends an appreciation of the past with an apprehension about the future of the natural world as we seek to dominate rather than understand God's great gift to us. Humor and irony permeate the essays, but each one carries an insight into human nature and the natural world we tend to take for granted. Bob carefully leads us to understand the roots of thoughtful conservation lie in the hard-learned lessons of our agricultural ancestors. A great read allowing us to laugh and ponder our place in the universe at the same time."

—**Dave Freudenthal,** Former Wyoming Governor

"Bob is smart, funny, and knowledgeable and his writing reflects that. True compassion for a landscape and a lifestyle. *Otters Dance* is worthwhile, a great addition to anyone's bookshelf."

—**Mary B. Flitner**, Author of *My Ranch, Too*

"I have always known growing up and living in Wyoming was one of the great blessings of my life. *Otters Dance* puts into words many of the reasons why it is such a blessing to have a Wyoming life. It is the scenery. It is the solitude. It is the wildlife, but perhaps more than anything, it is Wyoming people. Wyoming people—who are both rugged and respectful, practical and sentimental, who live each day to the fullest, while fully giving back to others and always striving to improve Wyoming for future generations.

"*Otters Dance* shares the magic and wonder of Wyoming through the eyes of one who knows that the state and her people are special. Bob Budd, with humor and humility shares his life lessons with a collection of stories that as a Wyoming ranch kid, reminded me of my childhood and why I love Wyoming and her people."

—**Matt Mead**, Former Wyoming Governor

"Between these covers await many lasting pleasures. Bob Budd writes like a poet and thinks like an ecologist. He has given us precious essays that entwine people and land—for the better. This book belongs on every reader's bookshelf."

—**Richard Knight**, Professor Emeritus of Wildlife Conservation, Colorado State University

"Humans are storytellers. We understand the world through stories. We place our lives within the context of stories. Bob Budd is a great storyteller. Every essay in *Otters Dance* reflects his deep appreciation for the diversity of people and landscapes we coinhabit with the whole of life on earth. Throughout the book, he challenges us to embrace one another and life in its myriad forms as we strive to coevolve within ever-changing social, economic, and ecological settings. In the end, he invites us to savor the mysteries and wonders of our ever-so-brief visit to this planet we call earth."

—**Fred Provenza**, Professor Emeritus at
Utah State University and Author of *Nourishment*

OTTERS DANCE

A RANCHER'S JOURNEY TO ENLIGHTENMENT AND STEWARDSHIP

BY

BOB BUDD

Fulcrum Publishing
Wheat Ridge, Colorado

All interior illustrations by Bob Budd.
Cover illustration and cover design by Kateri Kramer.

Library of Congress Cataloging-in-Publication Data

Names: Budd, Bob, author and illustrator.
Title: Otters dance : a rancher's journey to enlightenment and
    stewardship
    / Bob Budd ; illustrations by Bob Budd.
Other titles: Rancher's journey to enlightenment and stewardship
Description: Wheat Ridge, Colorado : Fulcrum Publishing, [2022]
Identifiers: LCCN 2022003878 | ISBN 9781682753408 (paperback)
Subjects: LCSH: Ranchers. | Sustainable agriculture. | Autobiographies.
Classification: LCC F765 .B826 2022 | DDC 636/.01092--dc23/
    eng/20220209
LC record available at https://lccn.loc.gov/2022003878

Printed in the United States
0 9 8 7 6 5 4 3 2 1

Fulcrum Publishing
3970 Youngfield Street
Wheat Ridge, Colorado 80033
(800) 992-2908 • (303) 277-1623
www.fulcrumbooks.com

For Lynn,
my one and only

CONTENTS

INTRODUCTION

I n August 1879, my great-great-grandfather boarded a train in Kansas and headed to Nevada. Seems his brother had bought a herd of cattle and died under suspicious circumstances in the process, so Daniel B. Budd went out to gather them up and bring them back. Simple as that. There were some obstacles. He had to find a crew that actually wanted to go to Kansas, then traverse 1,400 miles of desert and the Rocky Mountains, horseback, at the pace of a cow, straight into the teeth of winter.

Winter won, and Daniel B. and his crew worked the cattle up the Green River to Piney Creek, where they holed up in an abandoned trapper's cabin in the absolute middle of nowhere. When the days grew longer and the snowdrifts shorter, men and cattle had survived, and Daniel B. declared it a great place to winter. It is now known as the "Icebox of the Nation."

Five generations later, I was brought into this heritage, totally without my consent. Combined with my mother's family from across the Wind River Mountains, my earliest memories are a constant stream of aunts, uncles, cousins, mothers, and fathers and an assortment of other people who fit in somehow, somewhere. Most of my genealogy was passed down at brandings and funerals, and as a youngster, I learned quickly that you could learn a lot by just sitting near old folks and being willing to listen. And, you almost always got candy and extra pie.

My world was a community, though it took me years to understand that I had been given this incredible gift. There were lots of ranchers in that world, to be sure, but there were loggers and oilmen, artists and musicians, hunting guides, bankers, and politicians. There were teetotalers and drunks, teachers and salesmen, game wardens and truck drivers. There were lawmen and law breakers, soldiers and sailors and poets. Every one of them had a story, and most of the stories were fascinating. Hard work and hard play were mandatory, and the greatest sin was lying—"better to tell the truth and take a whipping than to lie and have to remember your bull-shit story" was a pretty common adage. Tall tales and legends were exempt from this rule—you were expected to know the damn difference.

There was one thing we all had in common, and that was an undying attachment to the land, the creeks, the swamps, and critters that made up the Piney country. And even as generations moved away, that attachment never waned. Instead, it became manifest in other places, other landscapes and creeks and wetlands and deserts. It lived on through hard work and hard play, through hunting and fishing and storytelling. And for me, it grew immensely, person by person, ranch by ranch, acre by acre, mile by mile.

A lot of college weekends were spent building fence, branding, stacking hay, shipping yearlings, and drinking beer. I came from rocky ground where it took hours to dig a posthole, and hours to tamp the posts in tight—I dug postholes in sand with nothing but a shovel, and set the posts by simply shaking them. I grew up where the summer was spent growing grass to cut and bale, so you could unbale it and put it back where it came from so cows and other critters could eat it—I found ranches where the wind blew the ridgetops clean and cows grazed all year long.

And, every single place I went from that day on, I found people who wanted to show me where the elk calved, and the cranes nested, and the bears denned. They didn't want to talk about cows, but they would—what they really wanted me to see was a creek full of fish, or a bobcat den, or a pond covered in green-winged teal. They wanted to talk about growing up in the country, about hard times and hard work, and good times—community.

So, slowly I absorbed the truth behind the ancient saying that "when the pupil is ready the teacher will appear," because it happened again and again. Looking backward, it became clear to me that when I was truly ready, teachers had emerged for all of my life. Looking forward, I found peace in the reality that the mentoring would never end, so long as I was open to new ideas and new knowledge. Shake not the knowledge of the past, and shirk not the knowledge of the future, for it is rare that they do not converge.

I had the greatest job in the world, representing the men and women in the ranching industry, driving every paved road and most of the dirt roads in Wyoming, a state where the footprint of nature was everywhere. I had mentors in every aspect of life, and I had a front row seat to the real world that lived off the beaten path. In many ways, it was like growing up on Piney Creek all over again, with longer rivers, deeper ponds, taller mountains, and different plants and animals. Every day held challenges, but every day was filled with opportunity and wonder.

In December 1993, my wife and I loaded up our three small children and made a much less treacherous journey than that of my great-great-grandfather a century before, to a ranch nestled at the base of the Wind River Mountains. We didn't face the same challenges he met in 1879, or we would have surely perished, but we did face a Wyoming winter, a landscape unfamiliar, and a new community. Ironically, the house we moved into was built in 1879.

And so began a new chapter, but like all of those before, this one was inextricably tied to soil and water, wildlife and native plants, cattle and horses, and a new community. Again, when I was ready, teachers emerged, sometimes in the strangest of places or situations. One wrong turn to buy hay led to a lifelong friendship and a mentor who was always there when I needed him. I met people from all walks of life and nearly every continent who shared a reverence and wonder for the natural world, and I was introduced to the concept of a radical center, where people looked for commonality instead of divisiveness.

This book is a collection of some of the things I have learned along the way. It is a collection of memories that come from the land, and the people who chose building community ahead of their own interests. I once asked a very diverse group of people to stand on a hillside and write down what they would like the valley below to look like in fifty years—despite their strongly held convictions, some diametrically opposite, their vision for the landscape of the future was identical. There are many more stories to tell from the past, and there will be more to come in the future, if we will just close our eyes, take a breath, and look for the many things we have in common, instead of those few that may divide us.

Oddly, I put the finishing touch to this introduction on paper at four o' clock on a Monday evening, and walked out to close up the shop at my parents' house. They still live on North Piney, just up the creek from the place where my great-great-grandfather hunkered down in 1879, and ulti-mately founded the town of Big Piney. They were down south, in a warmer place, and it was time to put the house to bed for a long winter. The sun was mostly gone; it was already dark enough to see moonlight reflect on snowflakes, a strange and wonderful moment that appears when day blends into night and cold blends into humidity. I backed the old truck into the shop (so when I had to jump-start it in the spring I could get to the battery), opened a beer, and heard a guttural "blaat" from outside.

I knew that sound, and as I stood in the doorway, a cow moose vaulted over the pole fence into the front yard. If she saw me, she didn't give a damn, and she headed for the flower bed in front of the house. Another call from her calf got her to stop, and she gave the youngster a look I recognized, shook her head, and knelt down to graze. The calf surveyed the top rail, ran down the fence, then back up, and down, and back to where I was standing, and launched himself into the yard. A young bull followed them, and the trio occupied the ground between the shop and the front door of the house.

I dug the last beer out of the cooler, closed up the shop, and walked around the house to sneak in the back door. I turned off the lights, the computer, and the TV, opened the windows, froze my ass off, and listened to the moose eat the last of my mother's summer flowers.

This was exactly where I was meant to be.

GRIFFEY HILL

The man sitting in the pickup was an accomplished hunter, mostly because he had a keen eye, and a sense of the country around him at all times. This day, he was hunting nothing, but as he drove down the hill outside town, movement on the escarpment called Griffey Hill caught his eye. He pulled over, grabbed his binoculars, and trained them on the nose of the rocky outcrop. There was nothing, but he was certain something had moved on that face.

He studied the landscape carefully, a seeming sheer face of rock that was in reality a series of sedimentary bands of sandstone outcrops and eroded sand. It was sheer enough, but not totally forbidding. He bet himself a cold beer that the movement had been a bobcat—the size was right, and nothing else would walk right up the nose of that barren scarp. Still, there was little reason for even a bobcat to scale the ridge, unless it caught the trail of a rabbit, and no rabbit had reason to be on a sandstone cliff. It didn't make sense.

He focused the binocs on the middle of the cliff, but there was no more motion. His best estimate pegged the distance from the valley floor at about 300 feet, maybe more. There was absolutely no reason for a bobcat to be anywhere on that hillside. He pulled the binoculars down, then saw the movement again, higher up the face of the ridge.

"Gotcha," he smiled, refocused the glasses, then let out a deep breath that turned into a hearty chuckle.

The figure in his lenses was a small boy, just about the size of a bobcat, in a filthy brown shirt and worn-out jeans. The boy had a crew cut and black glasses. His face was covered with freckles, and he looked to weigh about forty pounds, a little heavier than a bobcat. His feet were bound in a pair of "grundie" tennis shoes, the latest rage, and he was scaling the nose of the ridge, working back and forth across the sandstone, finding cracks in the rock, and shinnying his way to the top. At the base of the cliff lay a Sting-ray bicycle, obviously the boy's conveyance from the clutches of life in town.

The boy had reached the last shelf of sandrock, but when he reached out to the top, he suddenly jerked his right hand back from the capstone and sucked his gut to the face of the rock like a blue-bellied lizard. Very slowly, he pulled himself up the cliff, his hands in front of his chest now, digging his feet into the rock and inching his way upward. This time, he worked side to side, and his head rose slowly over the top of the caprock, until he hung on the face of the cliff like a horned toad, eyes focused on the shelf in front of him. He held himself there for a minute or more, then launched himself to the top of the hill and poked into the brush with a stick. And then, as if he had morphed from reptile to mule deer, he jumped off the cliff and slid, rolled, tumbled, jumped, and bounded back to the Sting-ray bike hundreds of feet below.

"You little shit," the man in the pickup laughed out loud. "Your dad will want to know about this."

* * *

That smallish boy with thick glasses and torn jeans was me. I was easily the smallest boy in my class and probably the most nearsighted as well. That particular face of Griffey Hill was the only one the big boys on motorcycles would never touch, and something inside me said that it was a challenge that I alone might conquer. I had climbed it before, many times, but never all the way to the top. Every trip, I learned a little more about the hill, and perhaps, a little more about myself. No two trips were ever the same.

This time, I had found the cliff an old friend, recognizing worn cracks and tiny holes in the sandstone, remembering little passages from one shelf to the other, zigzagging my way quickly past previous barriers. The final challenge was the caprock, a sandstone overhang that required me to climb up, then out, then up again. Falling was no great risk; I'd already fallen off the face more times than I could count. The first bounce was hard, but if I got my head up and feet down, it was a long slide to the bottom.

I had the cap figured by now. With my left hand anchored in a good crack right under the rim, and a good rest under each foot, all I needed was one lunge to get my right arm over the rock and pull myself up. I took a deep breath and made the move, but as soon as my arm hit the top of the rock,

I felt the scales and heard the buzz. I sucked my body back to the rock until I could catch my breath, trying to remember whether I felt the snake or heard it first, and fought the urge to jump. Mostly though, I wondered just how big that rattlesnake really was.

I poked my head back over the rim and the buzzing started as soon as my hair appeared. The snake had turned to the place where I grabbed it, and I could picture its black eyes, tongue darting for information, head back, on high alert.

I worked back to the left and poked my head up another time. Complete silence. I was staring directly at eleven rattles, a really, really big snake. I held my breath and myself up until I was sure I would fall off the cliff, and the snake slowly uncoiled and worked its way under a sagebrush farther up the hill. I caught a crack with my toe and another with my knee and I was on top of the hill, standing four feet tall and completely impervious to any form of adversity.

More than likely, I was late for supper, and in trouble again. No matter. I had climbed the nose of Griffey Hill and out-quicked a rattlesnake. I may have only weighed one stone, and stood the height of a sitting Labrador retriever, but I was *invincible*.

And then at dinner, right after I explained how the filth and shredded knees came from playing football in City Park, Dad informed me that a friend of his had called and told him he had seen me crawling up the nose of Griffey Hill like a lizard. He was worried that I might have been bitten by a rattlesnake.

At that moment, I understood that I was neither invincible, nor invisible. But, as I assured my father, I had outfoxed a rattlesnake. And, as far as anyone in the whole world knew, I was the only little bobcat who had ever scaled the nose of Griffey Hill and lived to tell the tale.

Maybe I really was invincible after all.

* * *

We all carry our world of sensual memories with us. Most are tiny bits of life unfelt when sensed. These pieces of our past are so incredibly powerful that a rainstorm in the night can take us beneath our bed, to hide from lightning forty years gone. One three-lobed leaf of sagebrush tucked into a letter is enough to transfer us from urban chaos to pristine prairie. The squeaking of a shovel into city sod reminds us of the first days of spring, when raging runoff from snows of winter is herded into ditches, and onto thirsty land.

These tiny things are conduits to the soul, a piece of ourselves that can neither be fully denied nor explained. In our depth, we must all have a connection to the land. It may be the feel of our feet on wet grass, soft sand, or warm water. Our connection to the land may come through a potted plant, or a pair of old shoes we wore when we hiked in Alaska. It may be an old family photograph—people cutting hay, branding calves, or having a picnic—and suddenly we feel the prickly awns of grass hay on our necks, smell burning hair, and taste the potato salad.

We are nothing more or less than the land we love, be it a city lot or the vast expanse of the plains. But, we need to temper our love of the land with an understanding of the landscapes we find most dear. It's in our nature to want things to remain just as they were when we first loved them. We relish the first time too much, whether the soft skin of lovers we touch, a flush of flowers on hillsides, or the taste of rain on the wind. We desperately want the past to be present, future to be past. We want to taste sensual memories all the time. We want to be important, and we want to live forever.

But, we are not eternal. We live a shorter life than many grasses, some mammals, and most trees. When we try to command natural processes that make the natural world work, we mess things up. Mountains erode. Valleys fill with silt. Grass is burned or eaten. Shit happens, and in the natural world, it happens in calamitous fashion most of the time.

* * *

This book is the accumulation of lessons taken from the people who have surrounded me and made me a better man. Some sat on barstools. Some talked best in the saddle, or the cab of a pickup. A few reclined in the governor's chair. Many passed through my life for reasons neither of us understood. All of them simply did what they believed in, day in and day out, and were happy to talk if only someone would ask and listen.

Most of my life lessons have come from ranchers. Almost every one of them tried to control nature at some point in their life, and nearly all determined that notion as foolish as the idea of "training" a wife. There have been many others along the way, miners and loggers, merchants and beggars, environmentalists, truck drivers and lawyers, artists and hermits. They are not uniform in their ethnicity, political party, intelligence, gender, age, or sexual preference.

The people who inspired this work hold three important constants. They are honest, sometimes to a fault. At the same time, they are patient and tolerant of new ideas. Most common to all of them is a deep reverence for the natural world, and the place humans occupy in that realm. We are part of the environment, and that will not change. At best, we are all learning organisms. At worst, we quit thinking and cease to challenge ourselves.

When you live a long way from the end of the pavement, you come to appreciate things you will never understand, and you come to revere them as much for the mystery as the elegance. In doing so, you honor your own short existence, and give way to those who come later to prove you both wrong and right. In doing so, you find not equilibrium, but balance. You find a way to remove chaos from your mind and leave it where it belongs . . . in the natural world.

Sometimes you walk home from the barn and stare at the dirt. Other times you walk home and see only the stars.

But always, you come home to the people you love.

THE WILLOWS

My father stopped in the middle of the road one day, growled at his grandsons, and pointed at a patch of willows as thick as the hair on a dog's back.

"We lost your dad one time, when he was knee-high to a grasshopper, and we finally found him way back in that patch of willows."

He drove on. Joe and Jake looked at me, and looked at their grandpa, and looked at each other.

"We lost that kid all the damn time," Grandpa shook his head. "If you weren't watching him, he was off in the creek or the chicken house or the meadow, but mostly, he was in the damn willows.

"Your grandmother would go apeshit. Grammy would grab her shotgun and head in one direction, and we would scour the place, but it was like looking for a damn needle in a haystack. He was only about three feet high, but he could run like a dang jackrabbit."

"How old was he?" one of the boys asked, looking at me like he had just found an arrowhead.

"Three or four," Grandpa said, "but it was the same when he was seven, or ten or twenty. We quit looking for him when he got to be about eight."

The willows were heaven then, and they remain that today. Sometimes, the lure was a frog that hopped and swam through the dozens of streams and ponds that flowed from beaver dams, muskrat holes, springs, and seeps. It may have been a bright yellow bird, or an owl, or maybe a rabbit that would never go in a hole. One time, it was a bobcat that snuck from the chicken house with a pullet in its mouth, then ran like hell. I followed the feathers until I could watch the bobcat eat the chicken, crunching the bones and shaking its head at the feathers. I wandered home, caught hell, and ate fried chicken. I said nothing about the bobcat.

Most of the time, the things I followed through the willows were deer. In the early 1960s, there was only one kind of deer on the creek—elegant, serene, silky-gray mule deer. The sight of a mule deer doe with fawns was, and remains, enough to decelerate the heartbeat and bring a smile. Maybe it was their huge ears, black eyes, or unique gait when they ran.

More likely, it was their graceful motion and their incredible, absolute grayness that evaporated into any landscape.

In the early morning, there were hundreds of them outside my window. They were in the yard, the meadows, and the road. They were in the sagebrush and the willows. Their breaths would puff as if they smoked cigarettes. By the time breakfast was over and the dishes were done, they were gone.

They were ghosts.

I had to know what they did all day. I wanted to sneak as ably and silently as they did through the willows, and touch them while they slept. I wanted to be invisible in sagebrush or willow. I wanted to jump six feet straight up into the air, disappear in an instant, then reappear behind myself, wind to my advantage.

I wanted to be a ghost.

It took some trying, but I got to the point where I could follow a doe and fawns as quietly as any human. My goal was to follow them until they chose a place to lie down for the day, and get back in time for breakfast, or maybe lunch. It helped to be knee-high to a grasshopper; I could slide under the willow branches with the deer and hide in the tall grass when they got nervous. Creek crossings were harder, sometimes too deep, but mostly too noisy. Before long, logs and rocks stationed in the creek allowed me to skip over the water in silence. By then, I knew most of the does by sight, and I could almost take a long circle and be waiting for them to bed down in their favorite places.

Now that I was a ghost, it really wasn't that much fun. It was perplexing, though. I could see groups of big buck deer in the morning, but I rarely found them in the willows. Once in a while, I would chase up a little buck, or a couple of them, but the really big deer seemed to be in the meadows early, then gone. Maybe I hadn't become a ghost at all.

"One time he walked about five miles," my dad told the boys. "He told his mother to get him up early so he could go out and follow the deer. He left the house and never came back for breakfast, or lunch. We sent out search parties and called the sheriff. He just disappeared."

"Where did you find him?" they asked.

"Aunt Pearl brought him home," Grandpa laughed. "He was about as dirty a kid as I ever saw, but he had a grin on his face from ear to ear."

The boys looked at me like they were the parent and I was the child.

"I just followed a group of buck deer to see where they went in the daytime," I shrugged.

There had been seven of them. Four were classic four-point bucks. Two were obviously younger, with three points on each side, but the last was the most spectacular deer I had ever seen. He was nearly the size of an elk it seemed, and his antlers spread beyond his shoulders. His muley ears looked small, and when he turned, I could see long, straight spikes over his eyes.

They grazed at the edge of the willows early, then began to disappear one at a time. One of the smaller bucks left the meadow first, followed quickly by one of the larger bucks, then another. It seemed like an eternity before the big buck left, head down, each step deliberate and strong. Within seconds of his cue, they all disappeared into the willows.

The herd worked their way upstream, never a sound, always within the cover of the taller brush. They left the willows and walked within twenty yards of my great-grandmother's window, then faded into sagebrush higher than a man's head. They stayed there for quite a while, and I had to follow them by watching under the tall sage for their legs. All at once, they jumped the fence and crossed the county road in a flash, into another patch of willows, where they followed an old streambed for at least a mile. It was clear to me now, they were headed to Dead Indian Dome, a long island of eroded sandstone about as barren and desolate as any part of the countryside.

I followed them to the base of the ridge, picking ticks off my arms and out of my hair, letting the flies bite without slapping. They didn't hurry, but there was no way I could keep up with the pace. I knew now that they had seen me, or smelled me, and they would hasten to cover, or leave the country all together. No problem. I knew where to find them.

I'm quite sure I knew by that time that I was the subject of the countywide search and rescue mission, so I made my way out of the sagebrush hills toward the safest place in the valley—Aunt Pearl's house. The problem with the trip was the changes in scenery. I found a pond full of pollywogs and captured enough to fill the bottom fold of my shirt, then analyzed them to see that some had begun to lose their gills, others displaying tiny little legs.

From the pond, I caught the tiniest glimpse of a sage chicken, scurrying to keep all her chicks within cackling distance. I figured I could catch one of the chicks and look it over, and I was right, but it took me in the opposite direction from

Aunt Pearl's, so I let the chick go and made my return to the safety behind my great-aunt's apron. Curiosity wouldn't kill me, but my mother might.

"What did Grandma do?" the boys both asked, as if on cue.

Grandpa laughed, a little chattering sound unique to him, and shook his head.

"Beats the hell outta' me," he said, "but, it didn't do any good."

He was right. I was obsessed with the detail I found in the thickets and bogs, incredible things completely unseen from only feet away. I could sit by the road, nearly touching the cars, and no one could see me. I waded into the muck in the summer, pulling out handfuls of freshwater shrimp. I found ways to shinny up a willow, to get a peek inside a hummingbird nest, and learned that when a cow moose comes after you, the best place to be is in the middle of the biggest willow. One day, my grandfather took me into the depths of the willows and showed me a wild rose with fifteen petals instead of five.

"Don't know why it's there," he said, "but it's pretty special, I think."

Pretty special, indeed. In retrospect, my forays into the depths of the willows was a gift, the honing of an ability to see the elegant intricacies of that world at a level beyond what I could find in books or see from the road. I could actually see differences between plants, habitats, and patterns of use by animals. Not until much, much later would those things be explained academically, sometimes not even then. At the time, it was osmotic, an absorption of my surroundings in a manner that continues today. I was learning to see a landscape as a living thing, the sum of many parts.

I graduated from the closeness of the thickets to another view as my own legs grew. By the time I was in my teens, I found myself drawn to the sandhill down the creek. From that vista, I could see the valley as a completely different creature, one made up of thousands of deer, hundreds of bogholes, and a gazillion pollywogs. I would try to imagine the folds and rises of the landscape, then walk into each to test what my eyes and brain told me was true.

I was always wrong.

Flatlands were, in reality, hummocked quagmires. Willow thickets were a series of individual lines, and between them were unseen patches of meadow and bog. Cottonwood forests were but stands of tall trees surrounded by sagebrush. Early light led to one conclusion. Evening glow led to another. And, in the dark of night, the willows were a completely different world, magical and frightening, a realm where my ears trumped my eyes.

Every season brought change, most subtle, but some sublime. The latter came mostly in the spring, when raging waters burst from the mountains and spread across the land. I would watch from the sandhill and launch myself into the valley below to see if I could find the subtleties, and explain the sublime. I had become a part of the landscape, if only as fickle as the songbirds that bred, fledged, and left every year, only to return when the sun and the water were high.

"How far did you walk?" Joe asked.

The question brought me back to the here and now, the part where I noticed a big grove of cottonwoods had fallen down. I determined to see if there were replacements coming back, or if that was the logical end of a remnant.

"I'm not sure," I said. "I just walked."

"It's about twelve miles from the sandhill to the Rathburn Place," Grandpa said, "if you draw a straight line."

He pulled up to the gate at the bottom of the sandhill, and I got out to pull it open. If the distance from there to the upper Rathburn was twelve miles as the crow flies, I must have walked a thousand miles as the weasel darts.

We crossed the creek and worked our way up the narrow road to the top of the hill, staring straight west into the setting sun, four sets of eyes fixed on the valley below. We knew for certain there were elk down there, somewhere, and we had four licenses.

Jake stared into his binoculars. Joe fingered the trigger of his rifle. Grandpa peered through a spotting scope fixed to his window. I sat in the sand, likely in one of my own buttprints, and scanned the terrain below us. I could feel a tick working its way up my leg, but I could get to him later.

The fallen cottonwoods would not be replaced. The creek had moved to the south, and rabbitbrush was slowly expanding onto the former stream bank below the old trees. A group of does and fawns were working their way into Cotton's meadow, and a beaver was cruising down the creek with dam material in its mouth. There was a porcupine so high in a willow that he was causing it to buck like a bronc. A cow moose and her calf crossed the creek behind the Beck House, and browsed on the willows. I followed the creek upstream with my eyes, and named the places in my mind, nearly every one of them named for a family long gone. Beck, Hughes, Muir, Lewis, Noble, Ott, Chrisman, Rathburn, Edwards, Guthrie, Fredell, another Rathburn. Twelve miles on a line. Maybe thirty if you followed the creek.

"See anything?" Grandpa whispered. Elk were on his mind, and the sun was falling like a stone. He was in no mood to hear about porcupines and muskrats. Dinner was waiting.

"No elk," I said.

We walked back to the truck and slid our rifles into their scabbards. Grandpa looked at his watch. I stared at the creek bottom. Joe and Jake looked at me.

"Tell Mom we'll be late for dinner," I said, and the boys and I headed down the sandhill, into the willows.

WHERE WILL
THE MOOSE LIVE?

There have been many defining moments in my life, and almost none of them seemed to be important at the time. A great single malt whiskey takes the right combination of peat smoke, chemical reaction, and time, lots of time. Really important things in life are usually the same way.

My grandparents lived in a small house on North Piney Creek, on an ancient gravel bar surrounded by floodplains that became hay meadows eighty years before I was born. The narrow lane to their house followed a ribbon of high ground between spring creeks and swamps, ending on an island of cobble with a house on top. It could take hours to dig a hole there.

The house was pretty typical for its time, built when a major generational shift overcame small ranches and farms. Small, practical, and inexpensive, the exterior was ringed by long lines of siding that surrounded the place like stripes on a skunk. Inside, the floors were all a single color of linoleum, and wallpaper covered thin layers of hard, pressed cardboard in most of the rooms. A large propane stove stood in the center of the house.

There were five rooms: a living room, kitchen, two bed-
rooms, and a bathroom. The warmest place in the house was the
bathroom, with an Arvin electric heater running full blast. You
entered the house from the south corner of the kitchen, unless
you had never been there. In that case you came in from the west,
through the front door. One night late, there came a scratching at
the front door, and Grandma answered it with a shotgun in her
hand. The caller was a pack rat hanging on the screen door, and
she blew it to smithereens from about three feet away. She also
blew the door to kingdom come.

All she said was "that son-of-a-bitch," like she had been
waiting to kill that rat all her life. I never came into the house
through that door again.

Everything happened in the kitchen anyway. It was a
huge room, lined full length on the east by windows, on the
north by a counter that was office for the ranch, and home for
jars of candy—black licorice, peppermint, and something called
horehound that all kids despised. The oven and sink were in
the northwest corner; on the west wall were a refrigerator and
freezer. The refrigerator held Hires root beer, and the freezer
stored Popsicles. The house smelled like the kitchen, and the
kitchen smelled like meat and potatoes.

For all of the sensory stimuli in that kitchen, the row of
windows on the east wall was magical. The roofline was low
enough that in some winters, only a sliver of light would sneak
between the roof and the snow on the ground. The sill was about
a foot high. If you looked evenly over the bottom sill, you could

see under trucks parked outside. In the winter, a smallish boy could look right up at the belly of a full-grown moose, identify the sex, and count the teats. More than often, the moose would look down, poke a broad nose at the top of the window, and steam it from the outside.

I was that smallish boy, and I was absolutely mesmerized by moose.

The moose is the largest member of the deer family, a gigantic, near-sighted, curious beast that appears ungainly and stupid. They were thick as mosquitoes on North Piney, and some winter mornings, I had to wait at the door while Grandpa shooed them away from the pickup. Depending on how much hay was left in the bed of the truck, there might be six or eight moose standing around, their breath combined into a great fog in the subzero air. Grandpa swept them away with a broom, as if they were gigantic metal shavings on the floor of the shop.

I asked everyone about moose. Were they really dumb? How come they were so tame? Should we name them? How many do you think live here? What do they eat in the summer? I harbored the notion I could climb out the window of my bedroom and ride one when they lay next to the house in the afternoons.

There were answers on the creek. If moose were dumb, they wouldn't be in the yard eating hay. They aren't tame—they just tolerate us. You don't give wild animals names—you give pets and people names. Moose eat moss and willows in the summer. You climb out that window and it will be the last ride of your life. Watch the cows with calves—they'll kill you quicker than lightning. If they chase you, get in the middle of the biggest willow on the creek and make yourself into a ball—they can't tear the whole willow apart. Don't try to outrun them—they may look awkward but they're really fast. Over time, I found almost every single thing I was told about moose was true.

Moose are truly an elegant and graceful creature, both agile and fast when need arises, but generally quite placid, almost tame. They are not a species of herds and mobs but instead tend to aggregate in smaller family groups. Moose have a fairly steady reproductive rate, and have twins when times are good, but it isn't unusual to find unbred cows, or cows with calves from two different years. They don't have a flight response like many large grazers, making them vulnerable to hunting. Moose are the ultimate of cool, the kings and queens of the bottomlands, more predator than prey to attackers. They may not be particularly handsome to some species, but they are quite attractive to one another.

Few other large animals are so completely defined by their habitat. Moose live in the narrow ribbons of rivers and streams that divide the sagebrush world of the West. While they may venture into timber and upland, they flourish in places where water is plentiful and out of control. They eat things that grow under the water, and they stand against tall willows to eat the tender growth at the tips of the branches. In the West, where settlement followed water and productive land, you can map moose habitat by cursive biological green lines, or square white lines of land ownership. In the end you have a species that is not particularly prolific, vulnerable to humans, and totally limited by a habitat that is primarily privately owned. Some would argue that such a species is doomed.

And yet, on North Piney, moose remained while other species declined. Mule deer were rare enough in the 1930s to merit excitement. Elk moved in and out of the valley with the seasons but stayed mainly in the higher elevations. Bighorn sheep were present above timberline, but not along the creek. Of all the species on North Piney, moose had the most to lose, yet persisted in the face of every natural and human variation. The anomaly was never a quandary. There wasn't so much intellectual need to explain everything at the time, and of course, moose were accepted, expected, and loved.

I got my first inkling why moose persist in an explosive confrontation in the early 1970s. My grandparents were in a financial crisis. The good economy of the 1940s and 1950s was over, and little ranches were falling apart. Both kids had left the place, and good help was nearly impossible to find. North Piney was experiencing only the third shift in generations in eighty years, but it would be much more painful than those before. A dead economy for ranchland and a vibrant market for every-thing you needed to keep a ranch going had people trapped. Suddenly, everyone focused on how to take a lot more out of the little bit they had. Calve earlier. Fertilize more. Sell calves instead of yearlings. Raise more hay. Kill sagebrush. Cut back. Buy land. Crossbreed. Sell land.

I could no longer look up at the belly of a moose from my gray-and-red, chrome-and-vinyl chair. Snow hid in the shad-ows of cottonwoods and willows, but the creek ran cloudy, water stood in the meadows, and bluebirds darted on the wind. In the kitchen, Grandpa sat and listened to a government man tell him how to kill the willows along the creek and create more hay-fields. The government would help. For every dollar Grandpa spent, they would kick in three.

Suddenly, my normally small, jocular grandfather burst from his chair and set upon the government man. Grandpa snarled and growled and jabbed at the man with his finger, then pushed and shoved him to the door and told him to get out and stay out. He was finally chased to his truck with the same broom Grandpa used to shoo away moose. In all my life, I had never seen Grandpa raise a hand to another person, ever. This time he was pissed.

Grandpa slammed the door and walked over to the stove. He poured a cup of coffee, and paced across the floor, an anxious, desperate, dance that went one way and then another and finally ended when he sank into a chair at the other end of the table. I followed his movement with my eyes, looked away when he looked at me, and studied the dark liquid in my cup. It isn't easy to see someone you admire go ballistic, and I had no idea what to expect next. Finally seated, he rubbed his eyes and his head, then let out a breath that whistled and wheezed. He crossed his legs and uncrossed them. He turned in his seat and looked out the windows. He tipped his head back and held his neck in his palms, and then he sat up and looked me square in the eye and shrugged.

"Where will the moose live?" he asked.

Where, indeed, will the moose live? My family helped to settle this valley, more than a century ago. They helped make the watershed a home for many. They carved a life from swamp and grass and sky and snow up to a tall man's ass. They cussed snow and they cussed drought and they cussed each other, and then they loved snow and each other. They learned to love wind and cold, and they sunk their own roots in the rocky ground and hung on to the place they knew and loved. And, if they hadn't loved moose, there would be no moose.

The only reason moose are still abundant on North Piney is that the people who live there want them there.

Aldo Leopold once said,

> There is no conceivable way by which the general
> public can legislate crabapples, or grape tangles, or
> plum thickets to grow up on these barren fence-
> rows, roadsides and slopes, nor will the resolutions
> or prayer of the city change the depth of next win-
> ter's snow nor cause cornshocks to be left in the
> fields to feed the birds. All the non-farming public
> can do is to provide information and build incen-
> tives on which farmers may act.

Gene Decker taught wildlife biology at Colorado State University for decades, and he tells anyone who will listen that the most important skill a wildlife biologist can learn is to "hunker." He demonstrates, squatting on his haunches and poking at the ground with a stick. He is adept at listening, a master of feeling the words and emotions of those with whom he hunkers. He has hunkered all over the world. He hunkers sometimes when he could sit in a chair. Gene has large ears, an open mind, and a heart the size of a moose.

Ultimately, conservation is vested in the heart. No amount of science, regulation, or wishing can make moose pop out of the bog. Conservation is sensual, and personal. Without the will to conserve, action lacks passion. Brain may connect with muscle, but blood still has to flow through the heart.

Conservation is not a battle. It is not the end game. There is no winner at the "end" of conservation. Conservation is always a means to an end. The result of conservation is three-dimensional, abstract, and often unknown. The glory lies only in the pursuit, never in the capture. When there are losers in conservation, the losers are usually everyone involved.

Conservation happens when things make sense. Things make sense when they do no harm or potentially improve on the existing situation, when they offer some source of satisfaction, without a sense of worry. Regulation, always based on "science," too often converts sensibility to threat. When that happens, the desire to conserve vanishes like cold breath in a hot kitchen. Statistics and science are important, but not when they create nagging worries in the minds of those on the land. Too many have been offered that chance to "kill the willows."

Conservation is driven by personal investment in the past and the future, and nothing inspires like the combination of heritage and succession. For most species, the combination of "here and now" gives way to the future only for brief moments of courtship, rut, and spawn. Humans have the capacity to move mentally in three dimensions. People on the land constantly weigh a sense of duty to the past with the needs of present and the hope of the future.

The frailty inherent in that ability comes when all dimensions play into a single moment. The bond to place is a hard knot, less often unwound than cut. When you leave a place you love, it is hard to go back. Decisions that change the place you love are no less painful. They are agonizing, and sometimes final. It matters little whether you are rancher, ranger, or game warden. Those who are new on the landscape must try to comprehend generations of duty, a season of drought, and a legacy left uncertain, sometimes all at once.

The temptation has become a tendency to resort to "science," rely on "statistics," and assume we are right. In doing so, we bypass the human element, the heart and soul that ultimately drives the survival of creatures like moose. If we really want to achieve landscape-scale conservation, we must first lose all vestiges of bias and disdain we learn through examples of failure. We have to learn to hunker. We have to grow bigger ears.

We have to comprehend the commitment of local people to the landscapes we wish to maintain.

The greatest challenge in wildlife conservation lies not in our ability to radio-collar and track moose on North Piney Creek. It is not our inability to accurately map moose habitat within meters of reality. We can model populations of moose and guess at their future output. We are especially good at understanding the things moose need to survive, but only recently has natural resource science begun to include the human element in the equation. For all the vagaries and nuances inherent in ecology and biology, understanding the attitudes of people toward species is even more complex.

Most people who work in conservation today didn't grow up in a kitchen on the creek where they work. Nearly all bring a combination of passion and good science to the table, but the focus is generally on science. For a period of time, we believed that was enough. We made decisions and recommendations based on today and the future, without appreciation and understanding of the past. In doing so, the knowledge and passion of those who live in the willows was lost or ignored.

At the same time, people on the land were dealing with a myriad of distractions—markets, weather, animal health, agency regulations, family, new agency personnel, new species, new ideas, new neighbors. Between 1980 and 1990, even the most progressive businesses struggled to deal with conversion from the IBM Selectric typewriter to the portable computer, from Volkswriter to Word Perfect to Microsoft Office. The explosion in communication and analytical process was unequaled, if not so spectacular as the transition from horse to spaceship seen by people still living on the creek, but it was much, much faster. The kitchen on North Piney still had a perfectly good manual typewriter on the counter, blank paper, and lots of pens in a jar, and all of a sudden, they were irrelevant.

Wildlife biologists were caught in the same vortex. People who built a career in the field were hit with paperwork and computer models and public hearings. The new idea was that "science" would answer every question. Congress wanted to hear about "science." The Supreme Court was interested in "science." Everyone was absorbed with science, as if suddenly the interest would make the natural world conform to the rigors of physics and chemistry. Surely, the combination of computers and science would prevail. Some used science in a manner that was openly hostile, arrogant, and demeaning, but mostly, it was meant to be helpful.

Up on North Piney, the moose missed the lecture.

So did the people who loved the moose. The lack of history by one partner collided with information overload in the other. It was as if one dancer heard a raucous jig while the other tried to count a waltz in their head. Only passion held them together, gave them the will to comprehend and accept different rhythms, and dance. But, in too many cases, the dance just ended. The music stopped. The community hall was empty. Passion gets dancers on the floor. After that, chemistry becomes much more than science.

The most critical thing we can do to conserve natural resources is to comprehend the past from people like those who love moose on North Piney Creek. All the computers and models and science in the world can't capture the passion and the understanding in the valley. You feel the land when you're on it every day. You find multiple tints of magenta in sunsets. You learn distinct hues of green on different species of willow. You see infinite shades of white in a drift of snow.

The human aspect of conservation is the most essential, and perhaps most ignored of all disciplines. Only in the past five to ten years has it even become accepted as a field of study. The collective knowledge of the people on the Piney creeks cannot be divined by modeling, wishing, or study. There is only one way to capture the wisdom of people, and that is by listening to them.

The best listening comes in warm kitchens on creeks where moose steam the windows with their breath. The human mind becomes three-dimensional at a table with a heritage. Most importantly, you begin to realize that there are real reasons for the things people do, for what they believe, and what they feel. Some of those reasons may be fragile, even unfounded, but they are reasons just the same, and they are important. Ultimately, few species can survive against the will of the people who live with them every day. Bobcats in the willows are welcomed; bobcats in the barn are not. Much of conservation lies in a delicate balance of mutual risk and faith.

The people you meet when your knees are under their table are an eclectic mix, and instantaneously shatter all images of who gets conservation done on the ground. There are octogenarians who never left the county, gazillionaires who have been there only for a few years, young couples trying like hell to resist the money of the city and raise their children close to the willows. Most are very well educated, and some are downright brilliant. When they find commonality in doing right by the land, you feel honored to sip their coffee.

Not long ago I asked four very different landowners on North Piney how the moose were doing. All told me first about a huge cow with twins, a moose that will likely be the comparison for all females to come. David had seen the big cow with twins the previous morning at the Lewis Place. Chad had run a dry cow and two little bulls from the Noble Place on Thursday. Cotton said there was a bull with antlers like a caribou down at the Beck Place, and he had a smaller cow with twins with him.

"That bull was up in my field this morning," Bill said, "but, he had a dry cow and a pair with him."

David had seen the dry cow between the Muir Place and the Noble Place the night before. She was coming in heat, he figured, and the caribou-looking bull must have chased the younger bulls off. Between the four of them, they had read about everything available on moose ecology, and they followed the animals with an intimacy generally saved for children. They knew most of them by sight, how many should be around, and where. I asked all four how many bulls were in the valley, about fifty square miles of country, and their estimates were uncannily close. When I wondered if that was enough bull moose, all said they would like to see more.

While questions are often addressed with incredible insight, suggestions about habitat improvement are commonly met with a quiet stare, no commitment, and questions. It is a common process, one that takes time to evaluate credibility, risks, and the reliability of making changes on the land. When those things make sense, the response is swift and anxious. Reverence for the past and commitment to the future become the present. The waltz becomes a jig.

One of the great frustrations in working in that setting lies in getting the step to the music right, at the right time. More often than not, landowners will take a very deliberate approach to conservation proposals at the outset, especially if they imply changes that may be detrimental. When those landowners decide to move forward, they suddenly hear an anxious backbeat, and wonder why their desire to dance is being ignored by others.

One family decided to place a conservation easement on their ranch after thinking about it for more than two years. In the space of that twenty-four months, one of the family might call about every six months. They searched the Web, read books, talked with their accountant, every member of the family, and anyone who might be able to shed light on every conceivable option. When they decided it was the right thing to do, they called weekly to see why it hadn't happened. They were worried, and they were anxious. Above all, they were excited about what they could do for a place they loved, their own home.

On the other end of the spectrum, conservation partners heard rock-and-roll from the beginning. The science said yes. The habitat was fantastic, thanks to the care of the family on the land, but its future was tenuous, vulnerable to being converted from ranch country and habitat to houses. The loss of families on the land was troubling. Agencies were ready to move when the sun came up in the morning. They interpreted hesitance as unwillingness and assumed they had lost the opportunity for conservation. By the time the family was ready to go, agency personnel were looking for funding, trying to get appraisals, biological assessments, seemingly moving to the drumbeat of a funeral dirge.

Every time you dance with someone new, it takes time to adjust to another set of muscles. Some hear the drum. Some hear the bass. Some hear a sound you cannot comprehend. You dance again for many reasons, but rarely in complete harmony. Mostly, you dance because you share a passion. Sometimes the passion is for each other. It may be the music, step, or the rhythm. There are also times when you dance because you both love something else.

We have made incredible advances in science and technology in the past few decades. We can build maps from outer space, or from palmtop computers on the back of a horse. We can track moose from deoxyribonucleic acid, ATVs, satellites, or moose poop.

Were I a moose on North Piney, I believe I would place my trust in Bill, Chad, David, and Cotton. I would stare into their kitchen windows and try to focus on smallish boys. I would hope like hell everyone at the table had the same passion for each other that they had for me.

BECK PLACE

The morning was damp, but not wet, hiding a chance of rain behind a razor thin layer of fog. The breath of the horses rose in tiny puffs of steam, then quickly warmed and disappeared. In the quiet of early light, the squawk of hinges on the metal gate seemed to reverberate through the valley. There would be no sneaking up on anything today.

The fields on either side of the two-track road were mown, hay gathered into stacks, grass nearly devoid of chlorophyll and now yellow brown. A little mule deer buck lay half hidden in the residue, his ears and eyes affixed to the pickup. A doe and fawn nibbled at the green base of the grasses to his left. Another group of deer lounged in the willows, leaves still hanging delicately, bright red and yellow. In the crisp air, the creek chuckled over rocks, low water hurrying to the river, and somewhere, a critter splashed through the water with little effort to conceal its presence.

The old red barn stood square as the day it was built. A new corner in the old corrals behind was evidence of care, if not enough deterrent to the dozen deer standing on the haystack inside. The barn could have used a coat of paint, but other than that and windows long broken, it was solid and functional.

An owl peered around one windowpane, as if annoyed to be aroused at such an indecent hour of day or night.

Once around the barn, the old Beck House stood like a grand forgotten sentinel, front door facing south, clattering open and shut. Two of the old corner posts from the yard were left standing, albeit askew, and out back, the screen around the meat house flapped from torn bottoms like the wings of so many buzzards. The outside, a mixture of plaster covering lath, was mostly intact, and high on the gable of the elegant upstairs, the old "PL Bar" brand was etched into the masonry.

The boys inquired about the brand. If they were the Becks, why not a "B" in the brand? What was the significance of the "PL"? Who had it now?

Their grandfather answered the questions he could, and shrugged his shoulders at the others. We parked where the old front gate had been.

"I ate a lot of big meals in that house," my dad said, "and they were quite the deal."

He described the meals—roasts and gravy, fried chicken, mashed potatoes, pies and cakes—and he described the reasons. There was branding, gathering, and shipping of cattle, haying, cutting firewood into chunks, ice into blocks. Holiday meals were the precursor to all-night sessions of cards.

"They were our closest neighbors," he remembered. That meant close enough for the women to walk, children to run. It seemed like the men would saddle a horse to go that far, maybe half a mile at the most. And, they did it often. There weren't any phones early on, and it got pretty lonely in one place all the time. The women would fish, and they were good at it. My grandmother, Dad's mom, would always get a hankering for fresh fish in the spring, and when the hankering hit, the fish were in peril.

"We fried a lot of fish in that old house," Dad laughed.

The boys and I looked through the broken windows. A bedframe stood crookedly in one room. The kitchen was ransacked, linoleum curling from the corners of the room. It reminded me of a rancher who once told me he had to choose between paying his association dues or getting his wife new linoleum in the kitchen. He'd been a member of the Cattlemen's Association for forty years, but with five years of price declines and rampant inflation, he had to make a choice. I had been to his place one time. It was about thirty miles from a paved road, and in the winter, he and his family would be there for months at a time, feeding cattle and watching it snow. Their kids were educated in a trailer house that served as a one-room school, even in the 1980s. I told him to get the linoleum and paid his dues myself.

Plaster had begun to fall from the ceiling and walls, an immediate victim when the roof began to leak. When first employed, plaster and lath was a shiny hard finish that resisted the worst of wear. I thought of Charles Rankin telling me about growing up in northeastern Wyoming. His father had ridden an immigrant train from the Midwest. He paid a fee to load his wagon, plow, stock, and self in a boxcar that unloaded him in the middle of the Thunder Basin, on a landscape slick with bentonite mud and so barren that one huge tract of land is still called the Lone Tree pasture. Charles remembered living in a tarpaper shack for years until they finally could afford a house with plaster and lath. Back then, it may have been more economically advantageous to ranch in a cold, harsh place than to be on the grasslands. It would have been an economy of snow, at a time when the cost of harvesting hay was low. The deeper the drifts, the longer the winter, the more water could be spread across meadows of long grass hay. Horses needed feeding, but they could pull a mower, push a plunger, or haul a sleigh. This was a time when the horses were harnessed almost daily, and they worked for their share of the long grasses. Out on the plains, any hay was a function of good fortune and rain at the right time. Cattlemen were limited as much by summer grazing as winter feed. Either way, the margins were razor thin.

Dad figured the house must have been built about 1925. It was there when he was a boy, and he was born in 1930. No one was still talking about the house being built that he could remember, and no one had enough money to build a house like that after 1929, so it had to be about eighty years old by now. Keep the doors closed and the screens on, and it wasn't all that ancient, really, even though it was made of pretty thin wood and pretty thick plaster.

A lot of the other frame houses in the valley were Sears and Roebuck kits that were shipped from Chicago on the railroad, then freighted from Opal on wagons, and built on the spot. The others were mostly log, with additions made of rough lumber sawed in nearly every draw on the mountain. There was only one other house like the Becks', and it was less than a mile away, the house my great-grandfather built, clearly at the same time the Beck House was built. The front porches and deep bay windows with quilted seats were too similar, but the brands carefully crafted right into the exterior plaster were unique. Were it not for the cottonwoods and willows fed by irrigation and flooding, you could have waved from house to house and seen the gesture.

There were only two doors to the outside on either house, one in the middle front, the other at the rear corner of the kitchen. The kitchen was situated at the back of the house, a functional design that put the cook only steps from the spring box, a seep sunk near the creek in this case, where water was available, cold and fresh every day. Off the same corner stood the meat house, a shaded gazebo in which whole animals and remainder parts hung most of the year without spoiling. The whole key to the meat house was keeping the screens absolutely tight. No flies, no sun, no problem. When I was little, I was given a hammer and tiny nails to pound into the wood strips that held the screens tight. As boys are wont to do, I saw a frog near the spring box, and followed another strategy for the day, then lied to my grandfather about the strips around the meat house. Within days, he hauled me into the screened enclosure and showed me meat blown by flies, then told me that was what we would eat for the rest of the week. Down at the Beck Place this day, forty years later, I would choose not to shoot a moose, for fear the meat would be ruined. They say the smell sticks with you forever. They're right.

My mind drifted to the other fancy house on the creek, and the days when I would leave my grandparents' home to visit my great-grandmother. It was about 200 yards from house to house, but the trail led through rye grasses six feet high in which lions, tigers, cobras, rabid skunks, bobcats, mean bulls, and dirty, thieving outlaws would hide. The trip was agonizing every time, and I would alternate strategies, running headlong one time, and sneaking the next, always arriving at the kitchen door in the nick of time. Grammy would be waiting, with a brown-and-orange sack of gingersnaps, a glass of fresh milk with real cream floating on the top, and stories. Every single time I went to her house, she would walk me to the front door and show me the place where I put my finger in the putty around the oval window before it was dry. Then she would cup my chin in her hands and stare at my eyes and proclaim them as "blue as a baby's." It meant something important to her. When she moved from that house years later, she took the door.

A single piece of lace curtain still hung from a corner of the living room window at the Beck Place. It seemed a white flag of sorts. Cows and other critters had broken through the old fir floors, and the feces of raccoons mostly, but other animals covered the floor.

"What is that?" Dad asked. "Is that coon shit?"

"Coon shit and cowshit," one of the boys said, unsure if they could really say "shit" in front of the man.

"There was never a raccoon on this creek when I grew up," their grandpa said, "and if I could trap like I used to, there wouldn't be another one of those shitting sons-of-bitches."

The boys relaxed, and the white lace fluttered, elegantly it seemed, catching the early light and dancing inside and outside the window. With the early light, and a house built to catch it, the room came alive. The window seats were suddenly warm and cozy, and the pieces of fir floor unbroken took on a luster that once shone with the elbow grease of lye and linseed oil.

"I remember dancing on this floor," Dad said.

I remembered the same kinds of things in the other house up the creek. The floors were hard and shined to perfection, with thick rugs and a hearty fire. I could recall curling up in bay windows in the morning, rugs at night, and I felt a sense of calm I hadn't felt in years. There was the smell of coffee and pipe smoke, the crackling of wood cut first on the mountain, then sawed into stove wood down the creek, at the Beck Place.

"They should tear these places down," Dad said. "They shouldn't be left to rot and fall apart. I ate here . . . a lot of times. I kissed a girl outside that kitchen door. I cut wood to burn in the fire. I remember Mrs. Beck showing us her new curtains. They were so happy here, and they were a part of this valley. If people aren't going to live in a house, they should tear the damn house down or burn it up. A house like this was never meant for cows and coons and pack rats. Get rid of it. Move on."

Those might have been the hardest words he ever put together. In one sense, he had to be willing to throw away his memories. In another, he had to embrace a future that was uncertain, one that might not recognize the challenges and choices people made at a different time, a time when some people disappeared, leaving only their names on the land they loved, or worse, leaving nothing. All cultures have faced these choices, and many have failed; those who persevere find a way to retain the old and welcome the new.

The boys and I pulled on jackets and hunting belts, slung rifles over shoulders, and disappeared into the willows. We heard the engine of the pickup grind back up the creek to a meeting place miles away where Grandpa would pick us up after the hunt. Within a hundred yards, I found both boys standing at the creek, staring through a clearing at the Beck Place.

"We should burn it down for Grandpa," the older son said. His brother nodded.

"It's not ours to burn down," I suggested.

"They wouldn't care," the older son continued. His theory held that the current owner was respectful of the original owner, and thus could not burn the house to the ground, but was not so respectful of the original owner that maintenance was a priority. This led to the conclusion that we would be doing the owner a "favor" by torching the historic house.

"Yeah," the younger son added, "and Grandpa would be really happy."

I sat on the creek bank and listened to them, and it occurred to me that we were staring at one of the best fishing holes on the place. I tried to think how many fish I'd caught there, beginning more than four decades before. The other hole, that open space in the willows, was a boggy place too wet for willows to grow, a low spot that served as a breeding ground for frogs and bugs. It took me more than forty years to see it, but the view from the Beck House looked right through that hole in the willows all the way to the Wyoming Range, twenty miles away. That house had been built to look right through that bog, up the creek to the mountains. Eighty years later, the view from the inside is still the same. There is a lot to be said for that.

As we worked our way through the tangle of willow and cottonwood, marshes, and sagebrush islands, I found myself looking back to the house. It seemed to follow me like the eye of a mother, that one she keeps in the back of her head. Was the Beck Place omnipresent? It sat on the sagebrush flank of a willowy jungle, yet stared into the heart of the mountains far behind. To the other side, the south, the view was hayfields, an ocean of grass. Beyond that sea, blue-green sagebrush hill-sides melted into desert mesas, and ninety miles from the Beck Place I could see the Wind River Mountains, the highest points in Wyoming.

Our hunt gained no glory. The boys turned down the deer they saw, deciding to wait for trophies, and I declined to shoot a moose. We followed a skunk for about half an hour, just to see what it would do, and we snuck up on a couple of big cutthroat trout. The younger son touched a porcupine on the nose on a dare from his brother, and then we all touched the nose until the porcupine climbed out of reach and scowled at us, tail fully armed and totally useless in the tangle of willow branches. We set our guns against a tree and crawled to the edge of the creek, sneaking up on ducks. At the end of the hunt, we stalked a trio of sandhill cranes to see how close we could get.

"I didn't hear any shooting," Grandpa said when we arrived.

"Nah," the boys said.

"See anything?" Grandpa asked.

"Not really," the younger son nodded.

"Hey Grandpa?" the older son asked. "Do you want us to burn that old house down for you?"

"Well," Grandpa laughed, "it isn't mine to burn down."

He looked at the boys, and he looked down the creek toward the Beck Place, the barn still tall and proud in the distance, house hidden by tall trees and willows.

"Other than the house, and the people, I guess the Beck Place is still pretty much the same as it was when I was your age," he smiled.

The ladies who cooked the meals and the cowboys who ate them are nearly all gone now. There are no girls left to kiss behind the kitchen in the dark. No trees have been hauled from the mountain to be cut into saw wood for decades. The sound and smell of the old workhorses that once filled the barn will never return. There is a hard leak in the kitchen corner, and plaster and lath is coming apart from the ceilings to the floors. Were it not for drought, the house would be in shambles. Now soon, rather than later, the house will collapse—once it starts, it doesn't take long. But the Beck Place is still the Beck Place, and it might remain the Beck Place for eternity.

From a pocket in his hunting coat, the younger grandson pulled out that one last fluttering piece of lace curtain from the front window and placed it in my father's hand.

"I wish we could have seen the old house back then," he said.

Dad looked back down the creek, and pointed to a notch in the Wind Rivers. He told the boys that in the morning, the sun would come up right between those two peaks, just like it did every day when he was their age.

"I wish you could have seen this valley then," he said, "but, it's really more important that the view from inside the old house is still the same today."

Somewhere else, there is a door with an oval window, a fingerprint in the hardened putty that spans generations. Hope remains.

PRETTY BLUE CAR

Like every family, mine has stories that are told again and again. Some are telling. Some are embarrassing. Some are funny. To the teller, they are always entertaining. To the object of the story, they become somewhat worn.

One story of my youth, about the "pretty blue car, all broke down," nearly wore me out, and now, almost fifty years later, it is still told at family events. As the tale goes, my grandfather, a superb horseman, took me to the corral to look at colts, one or more of which he was surely going to give me.

Instead of studying horseflesh, I stared outside the corral at a spent Ford sedan parked in the meadow, engine blown, wheels frozen in place. It was a color described as "robin egg blue." One door was closed. The other was open. The hood was closed but not latched, and the windows were mostly smashed. I was obsessed with the pretty blue car, all broke down, or as I supposedly said, "pwitty boo car awl bwoke down."

In 1960, this was not the making of a cowboy. As the oldest male in the next generation, I was not coming along very well. Even at the age of five or so, it was expected that I should be horseback, riding like the wind, not staring at a broken, useless machine.

Many of the ranches in the valley still used horses to hay, and nearly all fed hay in the winter with teams. Some kids still rode a horse to school. At the same time, nearly every ranch had a place for old cars and trucks that had met their maker (or their driver) and been parked, in the same manner that a dead animal was hauled to the "bone pile." This was the end of a mechanical revolution, a time when fully automated balers followed teams of horses cutting hay. It was a heady era, a time of hope, and a time of hubris.

To get to the pretty blue car, we drove over South Pass, in central Wyoming, on a route that circumvented an iron ore mine. Within peeing distance of the highway, the railroad tracks were littered with lost pellets of taconite—raw iron ore—headed to Pueblo, Colorado, to become fence posts, barbed wire, raw steel, and the basic elements of pretty blue cars. Somehow, I had to resolve this notion that we would dig something out of the ground on South Pass, turn it into little balls of iron, put those little balls on a train, cook them, shape them, turn them into a pretty blue car, and someday leave it all in a field outside a pen full of beautiful mares and their foals.

Within a few years, I had caught fish and hunted elk within earshot of the iron mine. I lost interest in the pretty blue car all broke down. I rode some of the colts in the corral, and I found great peace in myself when I was alone and outdoors. But, I was still mesmerized by the same connections that turned rocks into pretty blue cars.

But now, I was obsessed with mule deer, fish, weasels, moose, bobcats, and frogs.

At first, it seemed easier to comprehend the animals around me than the dirt-to-automobile connection. But, even natural things get complicated by reality pretty fast. Mule deer were highly mobile. I followed a group of bucks about five miles one day, from early morning in the meadow outside the house until they bedded in tall sagebrush beneath Dead Indian Dome. The sheriff was notified of my absence. I missed lunch and dinner. I would have made it home for dinner, but on my way back I saw a bobcat, and following a bobcat is a time-consuming effort. The sheriff couldn't track a bobcat worth a damn, but I damn sure could.

That bobcat cost the sheriff a hot supper. It cost me dinner and one hell of an ass-whipping. I figured I got the better end of the deal. I got to see the bobcat, and I knew where she lived.

In the morning, after a long, stern lecture about not leaving sight of the house, I headed up the creek to find the bobcat, and ran right into a cow moose with a little red calf, still wet and wobbly. I watched her for quite a while, until I heard some frogs croaking in the creek and followed the sound. I didn't see the frogs, but there was a mink hunting around, so I followed it down the creek a while, until it went into a hole and never came out.

Luckily, there was a mallard hen on the creek, and she had a brood of ducklings that I could follow through the grass. They were tiny and yellow, and easy enough to catch if I wanted to, but it was more fun to follow them. Suddenly, I was hungry, and I could see the house, so I went home.

I found out lunch was served in our house at noon, and only at noon, not at four o'clock (I also found out that Grandma could make a sandwich with lightning speed when no one else was looking, and I could eat it even faster). I found out the sheriff couldn't follow ducklings, but I damn sure could.

I was becoming something of a notorious criminal—a bobcat and duck chaser—a regular runaway train.

Those wanderings defined who I am, and in many ways, I think they are the elements that define all of us who live in Wyoming. First, I learned to pay attention to the slightest aberration, to think ahead, and anticipate logical transitions.

Some would call it "attention to detail," but I can assure you, it is nothing like that. I fail every single test given to find the extra letters in common words. I have to work like hell to balance a checkbook. But at the same time, I once found an arrowhead from a running horse. A single white shooting star stood out to me in a sea of purple.

Second, and more importantly, I gained an appreciation for the magnitude of the world around me, and that might be the most important aspect of those peregrinations through the willows. Aldo Leopold told us if we wanted to understand the natural world, we had to "think like a mountain." My favorite lesson from that classic is elementary: "just as a deer herd lives in mortal fear of its wolves, so does a mountain live in mortal fear of its deer."

In 1949, when that was published, the natural world was largely . . . natural. Now, sixty years later, the greatest challenge we face in conservation lies in maintaining natural processes in an unnatural world. How do we maintain catastrophe and recovery? What will it take to maintain migration routes and crucial habitats for wildlife? Will we be satisfied with remnant populations, wild zoos vulnerable to a single disturbance that once brought renewal?

It would be easy to confine this discussion to Jackson Hole, or Shirley Basin, or the Wyoming Range. We can lay out gloom-and-doom scenarios, insist that we draw lines in the sand and say no more. We could rally around a small population of sage grouse, or a pond full of dace, and make a stand, and in some cases, we should do that.

But, when we do, will we be looking at the pretty blue car all broke down, lamenting the decay of a single machine, while we miss the piss and vinegar of a crop of new foals behind us? Not every colt will play with your hair, or tug at your pockets. Sometimes, the best ones don't attract attention until you actually ride them.

Peeking outside this corner of the world, you quickly realize that many of the things we hold most dear are vulnerable to things we never anticipated. The trumpeter swan is an incredible example of dedication by a community, who became a source of birds that may again breed and return to habitats from Montana to Utah. Those are your birds. When we think like a mountain, they become all of our birds.

In the mid-1990s, I helped establish a bird-banding station on Red Canyon Ranch near Lander. More than 100 species of birds used less than forty acres. One yellow warbler was recaptured seven years later. This single bird, no more than a few ounces of her, had been back and forth to Central America or Mexico for nearly a decade. Standing in a market in Guadalajara in winter, I heard a wild bird sing. It was a yellow warbler. In the cage next to her, a meadowlark sang. I was tempted to buy the birds and release them, but chose not. It is one thing to rescue a bird from a cage in Guadalajara. It is another to give it a place to breed and nest. In the end, I would rather give the bird a chance to perpetuate than free it on an uncertain wind.

The hell of life is that we must sometimes cast fledglings on the wind and hope they find welcome habitats elsewhere. Our reach is longer than we think, even if it is only one step at a time. But, if we do not look outside our own backyard, we have no reach at all.

I have had the incredible experience of working in every county in this state. In every single little town, in every crossroads where native grass defines the skyline, and the skyline meets nothing but the sun every day, I have found a uniform reality. The common element is us, the people of Wyoming. We live here because of what we have, not because of what we have lost. We are optimists, and must be, for we live in a place most cannot either comprehend or tolerate.

Governor Mike Sullivan described Wyoming as nothing more than a large city with incredibly long streets. Annie

Proulx mined the underbelly and showed us neighborhoods we wanted to ignore. Jim Galvin lamented loss of community. John McPhee took us to our roots, to the very core of the landscape, to the people who are us. In our own neighborhoods, we may be alone, but when we become a community, we are incredible.

We have more sage grouse than any other state or province in the world. We have more Rocky Mountain bighorn sheep than any state. We have the most antelope in the world. We probably have more Shiras moose than all other states and provinces in North America combined. The black-footed ferret is alive today because it lives in Wyoming.

If we take care of sage grouse throughout the state, we will conserve seventy-three other species at the same time. If we maintain the ranches and bottomlands where moose thrive on the east slope of the Wyoming Range, we will positively influence 130 species of concern in the entire state—more than 80 percent of birds, nearly 70 percent of mammals, and half the amphibians considered vulnerable today.

In eastern Wyoming, we maintain the highest populations of swift fox in the world, in vast shortgrass prairie ecosystems lost to the rest of North America. These are some of the most spectacular vistas in the world, and some of the most biologically diverse. There is nothing in the world like a July monsoon just north of Cheyenne. On those days, sunsets simply cannot be replicated by Disney or Photoshop. These are days you can *smell*. The mountain plover lives here, an odd little bird that bobs about and nests on bare soil, a ruse so effective that it works to perfection. This is a bird that has been considered for listing as an endangered species, one that we can only care for when it is here. The mountain plover may illustrate our need for one another in an incomparable way.

Mountain plovers are drawn to large grazing animals for a variety of reasons. Since they nest on bare ground, they have a hardwired affinity for bison, cattle, and sheep. In the summer, they nest in areas where grazing is historically heavy, and in the winter, they seek out herds of animals that indicate forage. One of the most important areas for wintering plovers are the alfalfa fields of California, where sheep from the Great Basin winter. This species is tied to cattle in Wyoming, alfalfa in California, and sheep in Nevada. Break one link in the chain, and the species is vulnerable.

The chain is mostly intact, until you consider the price of converting alfalfa to houses in California. The market for alfalfa is tied to the market for late season forage for sheep from Nevada. Those who insist that the only way to save the desert tortoise in Nevada is to eliminate grazing in the Great Basin may serve to exterminate the mountain plover. We are all connected, and the species we love are connected to the things we do in our world.

My world is Wyoming. I have worked in Africa, Canada, China—all over the United States. I have stayed in tents and shacks, rondavels and fine hotels. I have tried to comprehend animals I have barely seen, in landscapes that are as foreign as my first trip into the willows. The challenges are always the same, and they inevitably come down to us.

Are we willing to wander from the yard and follow the deer, so that on our return we might find the bobcats? Will we risk dinner? When we look only at what we see, we see nothing more forever. When we see what we dream, we find focus. When we dream in front of others, we truly have a chance to make a difference.

Antelope that traverse the narrow red hills of the Gros Ventre, cross the Wind Rivers, and descend into the Green River Valley are a treasure for all of Wyoming. When we see that, we can evade the sheriff and follow the bobcat. Grandma will have a sandwich waiting when the time is right.

The pretty blue car is gone from the meadow outside the corral. The iron mine that made the pretty blue car is gone as well. The railroad tracks have been taken away, and the lost pellets of taconite are either picked up or trampled into the soil. Outside the corral, a moose and her blood-red calf remain.

CANARY
IN A WILLOW BUSH

Most years, bluebirds come home to Wyoming on the 23rd day of March. I know this date because I watched for bluebirds for decades on that very day, whether it falls on a weekend or in the middle of the week. It is not a date found in ornithological literature. The 23rd of March is my mother's birthday, and my mother loves bluebirds. Sons remember mothers, and the things that mothers love.

For a land manager, these little things become benchmarks, things to look for, like the first day snakes appear on the dusty hillsides, the last day snow lies drifted in the north pocket of the ridge. Scientists may show data to refute such "laws," and while managers may be impressed, data will not change the fact that bluebirds come to Wyoming on the 23rd of March. And, they will almost always appear in a snowstorm, flecks of sapphire blue against a field of sparkling diamonds.

In reality, there could be great argument about whether these blue birds are lazuli buntings, mountain bluebirds, eastern bluebirds, indigo buntings, or blue grosbeaks, but picking nits is best left to others. On the eastern slope of the Wind River Mountains, it is usually the buntings and the mountain bluebirds. In the Wyoming Range, it is almost always mountain bluebirds. In eastern Wyoming, the eastern bluebird is often the first one home. No matter where you find yourself on the high plains, a bluebird will appear in a snowstorm on my mother's birthday.

These benchmarks are important, and despite some of the silliness, they tend to keep our focus. Why bluebirds? Perhaps because they tend to arrive in concurrence with the calendar change from winter to spring, in a landscape where the second season lasts only a day or two. More likely it is their radiant cyanic color, something that is almost completely absent in terrestrial environments, save a handful of birds and the belly of lizards. After a lengthy season of browns and grays and constant snowfall, bluebirds in motion are as enticing as a swirling Mexican skirt.

I am not an ornithologist. I am not even a good bird-watcher. The birds I can recognize from their call are pretty much limited to goose, duck, meadowlark, and sandhill crane. If they hold really still, I can identify a lot of birds, or at least describe them enough to look them up later. I can tell a falcon from a buteo, but that has taken years. I've just always liked birds.

More than likely, that is imprinted upon me, like a gosling on a cat. I grew up with many wonderful, powerful women who absolutely loved birds. They were not well-educated in avian ecology, but when I was a little boy, my great-aunt would "sit" me at a bay window and shush me, then watch from the kitchen and tell me about each of the birds that fed at her handmade feeders, nested in the cracks of the cabin or the trees she planted close enough to see fledgings. Her favorites were wrens, but she cared not if the bird was brown or indigo. She was excited about every winged thing that appeared at her window. When we fished, she pointed to dippers, mergansers, and teal. When we drove to town, she counted sage grouse chicks, and verbally shooed kestrels and horned larks from the dusty road.

"Slow down!" she would bark, and she would glare at me with her schoolmarm eye, and I would slow down, even though the birds were quite safe. It took twice as long to go to town with Aunt Pearl, what with dodging birds and all.

My grandmother was a fan of the great horned owls that nested in a cottonwood outside her house for decades. My mother's mother loved wading birds and others that lived near the water. For Aunt Annie, it was desert birds. Aunt Sally adored rosy finches and other birds that were red. Each of them seemed to understand and accept the fact that these birds came and went with the snow, and each was content with their role in the lives of birds. None had control over the fate of these tiny visitors when they departed in the fall, and as much as they cared, they understood they had no mastery over things that fly.

The men in my early life also connected with birds, as much as they identified with plant and animal life. My grandfather called all yellow birds "canaries," and I still do that once in a while, if only to aggravate ornithologists. Grandpa had a high school education, a love for the land, and a great affection for canaries. He could tell a "black-winged canary" from a "yellow canary," and he adored both. One was a finch, the other a warbler. Some would hasten to point that out to him, and he would take that as an insult, a means of putting him in his place. What could be the point in correcting a man who grew willows for canaries, who understood where they lived, and defended those habitats in the face of "science" that told him otherwise?

We will not make the world a better place for birds by sharing graphs and data. We will not make habitat for birds by denigrating those who provide the habitat. We will make the world a better place for birds by engaging the innate sense people have for bright creatures in their lives, and by sharing a story of what these creatures need and like. Show a rancher a flycatcher and tell him what they need. Love knows no boundaries. Thickets will abound.

In order to care for the long-term welfare of birds, someone must understand the land and the places where birds live. When the birds are gone, somebody has to want them back. No amount of law, rule, regulation, or education will make that happen. Bright blue birds, canaries, curlews, and cranes become the means of commerce. The future of birds will be guided more by heart than law.

I am a land manager, and a rancher. I am a father, and a son. I am a husband, and a friend. My list of "favorite things" outside my family is pretty simple: bluebunch wheatgrass, river otters, rain, weasels, bobcats, mule deer, frogs, sedges, sagebrush, fish, falcons, fire, water, Idaho fescue, wolverines, bighorn sheep, pikas, swift foxes, willows, and hummingbirds. Tomorrow I will add other things I love. Nothing comes off the list. You either find ways to expand your heart, or your heart grows tired and stops.

I like rain and I hate drought, though both will always be a part of my world. I'm allergic to sagebrush, but I can't live without the smell. I like big systems, massive process, and all the little things that make time and space meaningful in the short term. I like diversity and accept chaos. I can live with natural systems in complete disarray. Stability comes more from change than stasis. One rain can make me or break me, depending on the day, the intensity, and the time of day. I try to think in geologic time, and act in my own time. I fully comprehend the paradox.

Birds are essential in my understanding of managing land, something I have only come to realize in recent years. Much more than background, sound, or color, birds offer some of the most important feedback to management of natural resources. In most cases, there is no need for detailed analysis. Presence or absence is often enough to help landowners manage for healthy ecosystems. Focusing on the positive, like canaries in the willows, is infectious, and personal.

Birds give land managers much more. They aren't just background and soundtrack to our work. Birds offer immediate insight and feedback to management of natural resources. And, like the proverbial "canary in the coal mine," birds can tell us things in a hurry. Relatively short life spans, and highly specialized habitat niches create a barometer of the landscape, or at a minimum, the vegetative landscape. For land managers, busy with a myriad of challenges, especially in the summer, color and sound is something easy to comprehend, and to act upon.

Ranchers and farmers are adept at seeing change, counting heads, and making the land better. Aldo Leopold said the public could do no more than "provide information and build incentives on which farmers may act." Positive returns come from positive messages. Sometimes, it is the simple things that make the greatest difference. Land managers will quickly pick up on the basics and adjust accordingly. A positive message will generate positive feedback.

The presence of American dippers in our streams is a credible indicator of water quality and a forage base for a species that is fairly picky about where it lives and eats. Other aquatic species, like kingfishers and blue herons, add information about the health of the stream. Flashes of yellow, whether goldfinch or yellow warbler, remind us that we are maintaining structure and density of woody plants that house and feed those birds and others. Willow and dusky flycatchers are great indicators of riparian health, while sage thrashers and Brewer's sparrows offer a clue to the condition of open sagebrush grasslands. Newcomers like blue grosbeaks and Bullock's orioles remind us that we have habitats for species slightly out of their normal range.

And sightings of birds less common help me remember the need for chaos that leads to a diversity of habitat types. For instance, as we have increased the scale and frequency of fire, we see Clark's nutcracker and other species that thrive in a dynamic system. Absence of some species may help us understand deficiencies of the system, or remind us that we need to maintain specific habitats because it is difficult to take joy in something that is missing. For landowners, the real, the here and now, will tell more than the maybe. As a result, indicators keyed to required habitats for many species are most desirable.

At Red Canyon Ranch, we were fortunate to have a banding station (MAPS) that is operating well into its second decade. From that meadow site, my learning curve has heightened and feedback to management is stronger and more constant. Andrea Orobona has been able to teach me in the field, at my pace. She and her helpers have captured ninety-six species of birds on that small sixty-acre site, mostly neotropical migrants. Those species and their habitat requirements guide management of the area.

The meadow is small, and rather than cut hay, we normally graze the area in early spring and late fall to allow ground-nesting birds a full season without disturbance. By moving cattle keyed to birds' reproductive needs, we have been able to reduce the number of captures of cowbirds, which indicates less potential for parasitism. We still remove the same amount of forage, but do so at times when we benefit by not feeding hay, or at times where the nutritional value of the grass is optimal to put on weight or improve condition of cattle. We have been able to expand willow and shrub habitat by reducing mechanical harvest of forage. By knowing our bird clientele, we have been able to develop a mix of grasses and forbs that best provides seeds of the size most beneficial to those species. When we do cut the meadow, we time it to allow birds to fledge. These are all management options that will work, not guided by all ninety-six species but rather by a handful of key residents that speak for the whole.

A yellow warbler was captured on the ranch last year that had been banded six years earlier. This year, a bird estimated to be six years old was recaptured. The fact that these birds have migrated successfully back to this ranch for six to eight years is not only astounding but also an indicator that our management should not be altered greatly in the near future.

The next step for avian biologists and ranchers is to develop simple, abbreviated guides to different ecosystems and types, based on the birds we see. While most ranchers do not

discuss warblers at peer meetings, they are universally drawn to birds and are truly curious about what birds tell them about the sustainability of their own ranches. Bird books are impressive, but intimidating. Song guides are helpful, but only if there are not too many notes in the tune. By making identification simple and correlating color and song with habitat and management, we will quickly see results on the ground. Results will be even more prevalent where mandate and regulation are absent.

The issues facing birds are the same issues facing land managers. Large habitat bases are being lost to rural subdivision and other alternative uses of the landscape. Habitat fragmentation and loss of large, open ranching landscapes are real and prevalent threats for many species. By using the responses of birds to guide our management of habitats, we will be able to sustain many species, and provide color and sound for those who love "bluebirds" and "canaries."

ROCK IN THE RIVER

W hen the Ice Age quit the Piney country, it left seed in sharp canyons and alpine flats of the Wind River Mountains, dark places where the sun passes only fleetingly. Glaciers feed streams, and creeks feed rivers below, and when you stand rivets-deep in your jeans at daylight, you gain a certain appreciation for the longevity of glaciers. In the rapids, an occasional burst of water would catch me in the small of the back, then follow a passage back to the river—between my legs.

My fly drifted quickly through white water—a gentle tug and the leader curled and brought the line into a turbid pool next to the bank. Beneath large willows, black water showed a flash of gold—a big brown. I raised the tip of the rod—too late. I swore under my breath and gathered line. Fish were active, feeding on minnows, grasshoppers, and six-legged critters that found water to their liking. Even with all the flashes of color and interest, I hadn't caught but one lazy rainbow that waited too long. I caught that one at daybreak, from the bank, and released it into white water and foam of the Green River.

Downstream, my fishing partner was ankle deep in the river, fish sack heavy on his shoulder. He'd landed a brown that had to weigh five pounds, a cutthroat nearly as big, and now he was bent over, stalking fish. His fly didn't need to drift. His arm arced out to the side, and he slid the line under the overhanging willows twice, floated the fly six inches over the surface of the water, snapped his wrist, and made the fly hover before settling. It was more than fish could stand. Water rolled, then erupted, and another huge cutthroat was on the run. He played her through the rapids into a big pool downstream and let her run. Normally, he would work the fish slowly, but this time, he followed quickly, wading in deeper to meet her halfway. He switched the rod to his left hand and bent to the fish with his right. As gently as he would lift his grandsons, he caressed the big cutthroat, slid the fly from her mouth, and let her tail slip through his hands.

I knew he'd caught his limit. I'd fished with him since I could stand in running water, and Dad never let fish go unless he had a sackful. For that he made no apology. Being raised in the Depression, he'd never gotten over the notion that fish were food, and every one was ultimately eaten, whether fried, dried, smoked, pickled, baked, or ground for burger. Food was food, but the law was the law. Catch a full sack by breakfast, and fish the rest of the day for the fun of it. Watching him taught me about competition, struggle, challenge. He stalked trout, and gave no quarter, but he touched each fish with the wonder of a child holding a snake.

He fished the other side of the fantail, and with his first cast, the rod tip bounced hard. I climbed on a big rock and watched the battle play out. Dad would move toward the bank with the fish, then slip and trip through the rocks, back to the middle of the river. He had the big fish close, then another run into dark water brought the rod up high. Finally, man and fish met in water that sloshed at the top of Dad's waders, and he reached down to slip the fly free.

"Good one," I yelled.

"Big brown," he yelled back. "Seven, maybe eight pounds!"

Behind me, the river roared, and the sun moved to a place where it would warm my back. Dad squinted in the glare, then pulled his hat lower over his eyes. The old silver belly Stetson was wrinkled and grayed, ring of grime around the band, mixture even parts sweat and hair oil. Beneath the hat, his hair was still curly, especially at the temples, where remnants of coal black hair were left from boyhood. He held a hand up to shade the sunrise, green eyes glowing from behind crow's feet and deep ravines in his brown hide. His face looked like a glove that fit just right. He walked upriver to the place where I perched.

"Catch anything?" he asked.

I shook my head.

"What the hell. You don't keep 'em anyway."

The sun had dried the tail of my shirt, and I shoved it into my jeans that it might warm my cold butt.

"Get any hits?" he wondered. His voice betrayed a certain disgust that his own flesh and blood might be unable to fend for himself in a stream so obviously filled with trout.

"I got a few."

"What are you using?" he asked, and his eyes drifted toward the end of my leader.

"Olive woolly worm."

"And you didn't catch anything?"

"Caught one early on."

"Oh, for hell sake," he scoffed, and he pointed his rod at the hole I'd just fished. "Oughta' be a good one in there."

"There is."

He sat on a rock and rolled his waders back.

"What're you using?" I asked. I knew the answer would be an olive woolly. If I'd had a caddis on, he'd have told me a caddis. It didn't matter what he used, and it didn't matter what I used. The man hunted fish. I spent my time looking for otters and mink, moose and birds. Fishing was my ticket to not work. To him, fishing was working, even when he had to let them go.

"I caught that big one on an olive woolly worm," he said. "Caught a couple others on a royal coachman. Had a big rainbow on a pheasant tail. Hell, it doesn't matter what you use here. They'll bite a steel ball if you throw it at 'em."

There it was! I hadn't tried a goddamn steel ball! What a dumbass I must have been. I just grinned and stared at my feet.

"You need to use less wrist and more arm," he decided. "You don't get that rod tip up when you've got a hit. That's the problem."

I stood up to let the sun dry my jeans, and he squinted at me.

"Why don't you get a pair of irrigating boots?"

"I like the feel of the water."

"That's bullshit. I'll loan you my old boots, but you oughta' get a pair of your own."

"I don't need rubber boots to make me a fisherman," I said. "I need to spend more time fishing."

"As much time as you need, you'd best get some boots. You'll be wrinkled up like a raisin before you catch anything."

It was the same give and take we'd tossed back and forth since I was old enough to talk. I liked it when he jabbed my ass, and while he would never admit it, he liked to get it back. It was practice, and there were rules, though they were never outlined. Last word went to him, unless I really hit a good lick. When that did happen, he would just grin.

I'd made a study of the man, I realized, and lately, he'd begun to treat me more like he did his fishing buddies. Mostly that was a constant stream of bullshit and abuse. In his mind, he hadn't changed the way he treated me one bit. In mine, every-thing was different. Only now did it occur to me that maybe he tried to treat me like a man too soon. He could sustain a level of bullshit, banter, and discussion for hours on end with men his age, but he grew impatient with me and pulled out early. Maybe now, he was trying to treat me less like a man and more like that child he taught to be a man too early.

The lure of the pool I'd fished overcame him, and from his seat on the boulder he floated a caddis delicately beneath the canopy of a willow. As soon as the fly settled on water, a big brown hit. Dad worked it to the rock where he was sitting, but the fish had taken the fly deep in its throat. Dad held the rod beneath his arm, dug out his pocketknife, and cut the line. The hook would work its way out in a day or two, fish none the worse for the experience, but I knew it galled Dad to lose a fly that cost six bits. God knows, I'd seen him catch fish on flies that had the hackles eaten clean off, not much more than a bare hook.

We'd fished a lot of water over the years, most of it the same reaches of stream and river at different times. We hadn't the wherewithal to fish Patagonia, New Zealand, Nova Scotia, and other places we dreamed about, but we had gained a sense of understanding of rivers like the Green, and hundreds of small streams, some without names. Even then, we were a far cry from the professional fishing guides who sensed fish from ambient temperature and types of clouds. Dad could get his fly figured out in two or three shots, but I could throw my whole collection without so much as a look from fish. Being on the river wasn't about fish. It was about people.

"What do you suppose will happen to this country?" I asked.

"Beats the hell out of me," he said. "In a lot of ways, I wish it would go back to what it was, and in others, I'm alright with letting your generation sort it out. I don't envy you, though. When everybody was broke, it was pretty easy to decide what was important. Now, it seems like everybody has lots of money, but no focus."

He was born in 1930, and he came of age in a world of economic depression, drought, and war. He told us about getting sugar at Christmas, and only at Christmas. It was obviously impressionable, because my recollections about him getting sugar at Christmas came in tandem with every candy bar I ever ate as a child. I still eat very little candy because Dad only got sugar at Christmas. Dad rode a horse to a one-room school, in a huge county where everyone knew each other. He remembered the first car on North Piney Creek, and he knew where it was parked, right where it died in a boghole seventy years before.

I grew up walking to a modern school, in a town where people came and went, and many didn't know the name of their next-door neighbor. I thought "Fibber and Molly" were the team of Belgians my grandfather had, until somebody told me about the radio show. We had color television, eight-track players, and access to boats, snowmobiles, and carnival rides. On the bank of the river sat the fourth pickup I'd had in little more than a decade.

Dad sat on the rock with me, and we said nothing. Water and air moved around us, each with its own sound, and the sun rose higher, taking shadows from the pools, chasing fish into the margins of the river. A pair of sandhill cranes appeared overhead, their strange sound seeming to echo off thin air. We watched them descend beyond the willows, and I found myself thinking about those stupid waders.

I had a pair of irrigating boots. They were about a month old, and the reason I wasn't wearing them was that the left one had a hole that I had never repaired, and it was quicker and easier to fish in tennis shoes than fix my boots. I looked at the boots on Dad. The old guys in the valley kept a pair of waders for years, until patches covered patches, and the rubber underneath just wore out. Then, they were amazed to find that a pair of waders cost more than the last time they bought them. I vowed to find that hole and fix my boots when I got home.

I didn't have the patience to patch a pair of boots, in part because my mind seemed to race at a dangerous speed. I wanted to understand what was happening in the valley, what had led us there, where the world was going. I was trapped by the notion that I had to figure it out in my lifetime, self-absorbed by my own importance, and terrified by the idea that maybe I would never understand what was happening.

"You won't figure everything out on one fishing trip," Dad said out of the blue.

It was another of his observations. He tossed them out like a hatch of mayflies, not there one minute, and abundant the next. Thousands of little tidbits like this accumulated in my mind, little snippets of truth handed out over three decades and three generations, and they were driving me nuts.

Not long before this day, at a funeral, I asked all the old-timers what the biggest change in the country in their lifetimes was. I'd anticipated a series of tales to be unloaded, pontification, and debate. I expected to hear how us young pups didn't know shit, and the whole world would collapse with the next funeral. Surely there would be some shots fired at the fact that I had long, curly hair like a girl. It didn't happen that way. The old-timers frowned, stared at their boots, looked at each other, grunted and scratched a bit, until one and all looked right at me. The oldest of them turned his head a little bit and spoke.

"There was more water," he said, and the others nodded.

I was speechless. If a hog had walked in the yard and eaten one of us, this group of men would have argued whether it was a dog or a goat that did the deed. They would have laid bets on who owned the hog, and then they would have shot and cooked the son-of-a-bitch, insisting all the while that it was an elephant. These guys never agreed to anything, and here they were telling me in a singular voice that there was one major change in the valley over the course of nearly a century. I didn't want to hear that answer. I wanted to hear lots of answers.

"You need a haircut," Dad brought me back to the rock in the middle of the river. "Pisses your mother and your sisters off that you have all those curls."

"Was there really more water when you were a kid?" I asked.

"There was more water when *you* were a kid," he answered.

He talked on, and I tried again to put the pieces together. The deer were almost hunted to nothing when he was a boy. No raccoons or foxes were in the valley. Bobcats were common. There were so many sage chickens that haying crews went on strike before they would eat another. Nobody had heard a sand-hill crane.

"You want lunch?" Dad asked, and I agreed to the idea. Dad dug around in his fish sack, fish slime on his hand and sleeve, intent on fetching out some sumptuous treats to eat. I'd been to this restaurant before.

"Got any Vienna sausages in there?" I asked.

"You got a problem with Vienna sausages?" he asked.

"Not at all," I said.

Out came two cans of the finest sausages ever canned in Vienna, followed by a tin of sardines in ketchup. A sleeve of crumbled crackers followed, and for vegetables, he had a can of green olives, stuffed with pimentos. With some flourish, he added the final course, a can of smoked oysters.

"No Spam?" I asked.

He took a deep breath and shoved a sausage and some cracker crumbs in his mouth. I wondered how many times he'd taken that same deep breath, and decided I didn't really want to know. I ate a Vienna sausage and actually enjoyed it. I hogged the oysters when he wasn't looking. Tried a ketchup sardine and hated it. Mostly I sat and realized that I loved this man more than anything in the world. I loved him for his passion that made me crazy, and I loved him for his ways that I could never understand, and I loved him for the things he had taught me by not lecturing me.

More than anything else, I needed to make this day a lesson he taught without knowing he was teaching. I needed something I didn't understand. I needed the connection that would make sense of people, place, and natural process. I didn't need data. I needed facts.

Most of the facts were already there. Families in the Piney
country had stayed in spite of the weather and other challenges.
But, the country had changed, and in many ways the change
was immense, greater than the sum of its parts. Obviously, the
town changed, as did the people, and the color of the cattle. But
the land had changed. It seemed incomprehensible that a world
shaped by geologic time could become so different in less than
a century.

In the short term, changes were almost always dis-
missed in simplistic terms. It was the drought, or the flood,
or grazing, or logging, or some whipping boy of the moment.
At this time in the valley, most problems were deemed to be
the direct result of Jimmy Carter being elected president. In
the mainstream, issues were addressed as if each was a single practice, a constant influence on the land, with the ability
to debilitate the environment overnight. Claims and realities
were inconsistent. On the surface of the earth, ranching was
highly variable and had changed immensely over the course of
a century. There were far less cattle than when Dad was young,
and still the land had changed. The most constant element in
ranching in the valley was the people who calved the cows. But
the changes in ranching were minor.

People were more mobile, more wealthy, and less busy.
They could be almost anywhere instantly. I rode a horse into
North Piney Lake as a boy and walked there as a young man. It
took about four hours either way. Now, on a hopped-up Husq-
varna motorcycle, it was a half-hour ride.

In the yard of the old ranch stood an amalgamation of iron—gears, wheels, blades, and beams—that made up an old horse-drawn road grader. On a good day back then, you could work up a couple miles of six-foot road. Now, the county blade hand could cover ten miles of twenty-foot road in a morning.

"Other than the water, what was the biggest change in the country?" I asked Dad.

"Jimmy Carter," he said, and then he laughed like hell. He threw a fly into the river out of habit, and nervousness, and a fish rose to meet his cast in the middle of the day. He played the fish to the rock and let it go.

"There were a lot more people then," he said, "and a lot less houses."

He painted the picture by name. Nearly every canyon and draw on the mountain had a sawmill. One was his mother's father's mill. Over the hill, another family cut trees and fashioned them into rough lumber. On one little ranch up Middle Piney, there were two Sawmill Canyons. Even now, you could look at a topographic map and find a little black square in most drainages, marked only with the word "sawmill." The buildings on most ranches were an assortment of boards cut on the mountain and hauled to the valley in wagons. A whole lot of families could make boards and not make a lot of holes in the forest.

Other than around the hay meadows, there wasn't a fence in the country, except the one that runs below Bench Corral Springs. When all the cattle came together there were a couple thousand head. They worked the cattle on the flat west of Big Piney, sorting the pairs from the yearlings, working them toward the drift fence and the day when the roundup crew took over. Cows and calves went one way, and the yearlings and two-year-olds went to the high country. Some people worked the roundup. Some tended cows and calves. Others cut the hay.

A battered Chevy pickup rattled over the highway bridge in the distance, in the bed an anxious border collie. A left arm poked out the driver's side window, and Dad raised an arm in return.

"One of the Sommerses," he said, "probably young Albert." Another vehicle rounded the corner and slowed on the bridge. This one had a kayak attached to the top, and a sled dog slobbering out the back window.

"Beats the shit out of me," Dad shrugged, but he waved anyway.

"We had a community," he said. "We had each other. We had each other to love, and we had each other to hate, but we had each other, and that was worth a lot. I got drunk one time on beer a man bought me, and his wife told my mother I was drinking. It was quite an elegant balance, but it worked."

I stared down the river, imagining a place so intimate, and realized I lived in that world. I might absorb the sins of the father, but I was accorded the innocence of youth. If I had a shred of integrity, I would find the sins of the father less compelling than the deference to indiscretion. There is an intricate beauty in waving to all the cars on the bridge.

Dad slid off the rock into the water as deftly as if he was a muskrat or an otter, headed for the truck.

"I can't tell you what to do from here," he said, "but I have faith that you'll try to do what is right for your generation. That's about all I can offer."

I slid into the river behind him, and the cold water hit my warm, dry jeans and made me gasp enough that he could hear it out loud. He turned and looked at me, his face torn between respect, despair, and amusement.

Wading across the river where I'd grown up, I suddenly realized everything was about people. Every good choice I'd made was influenced by people, and every bad one was the same.

"I need to patch those boots," I suggested.

"I patched your boots last night," Dad said. "You need a haircut."

COLORS AND WORDS

R anchers talk in questions—arm-out-pickup-window, elbow-on-saddle-horn, head-scratching, cap-moving, hat-adjusting, dirt-digging-with-toe-of-old-boot questions. It's just easier to start a conversation with a question than an answer. Questions can be simple, innocuous, as bland as observations on weather, but they are often deeper, harder, and impossible to answer directly. When you talk in questions, sanity can remain intact. Answers are sometimes certain death—of mind, heart, and bottom line.

"Suppose a guy was really worried about losing his place? He had a note at the bank, say, and he was in pretty good shape on the land, and he could cover the operating note with fifty more mama cows, but he hasn't got enough summer country. He can winter more cows, but he can't do that if the cows are coming off his summer country in August. Now, suppose a place that makes his ranch *really* work good comes up for sale, but the price is for houses? I hear some of that stuff is going for three thousand an acre. Maybe it's only two thousand, but cows make it a hundred at best, don't you think? So what do you tell that feller to do? Sell out? Or buy land high and lose it later?"

Sometimes the questions can get sort of long and com plicated. This may be the curse of an open mind, or the agony of too much tradition. Simple statements end with a rising pitch, as if to place a question mark where none would normally be found. This is a relic of reality, of swings in weather that drive the thermometer one hundred degrees in hours. Speaking in questions is a simple reflection of people who live on the land. We don't know as much about this landscape as we wish, and we learn through questions. We can say with certainty and honor that we don't know all the answers, and we can say with equal certainty that simple solutions in a complex landscape are prone to failure.

Dave Gardner, a rancher friend, was aggravated by a particularly long dry spell when he was a younger man. In frustration he asked his father-in-law, a Shoshone elder, if he thought it would ever rain.

"It always has," was the answer.

Reality can be hard to live with. Some pray for rain while others relish reports that the weekend will be "great— dry and warm." In ranching, reality has a way of burning itself into a man's hide, creating a paradox of pessimism on the out- side and blatant optimism on the inside that it will, indeed, rain. Management of natural lands requires the patience of glaciers and the ability to rebuild a framework from pieces scattered on the ground. Ranching is built as much on appre- ciation of decay as on lush grass in springtime. In our human obsession to control everything, we err by hoping for stability where chaos rules. Successful ranchers manage for a range of options, from drought to perfect moisture regimes, and then adapt, and adapt, and adapt.

The culture of ranching is a dichotomy of certain knowledge and total acceptance of random chance. In a "normal year" cows do certain things. Grass grows a certain way. Hay produces. Deer behave the normal way. But a normal year is a moving average, built on how many years the rancher has lived on a piece of land. In business circles and culture, the term "adaptive management" has become the buzz. In a century and a half of ranching, no one ever thought to coin the phrase because they were too damn busy adapting.

Of late it seems ranching is counterculture at its apex, out of step with the mindset of the time. When the national passion was farming and settlement, ranching was some sort of fanciful retrogression to nomadic days of following grass and water. John Iliff herded cattle from the safety of the Colorado plains into the heartland of Wyoming. Charlie Goodnight followed grass to Montana. Pan Phillips and Rich Hobson chased grass beyond the mountains to British Columbia. Like a colt in halter, there was a great deal of pulling back and lurching forward.

Society said settle down, make a go on a single piece of ground, build a town. Stay put. Hunker down. But instinct said follow grass. Maybe early ranchers had more in common with the Crow and Shoshone than they did with plow and post.

Suddenly ranching epitomizes sense of place: units of land that hold vast landscapes of the West together. But one ranch alone can't support the frame any more than a single nail can anchor four boards around a photo of the past. Ranching has been depicted as a world of lonely independence, cocksure and superior wisdom lined up in the face of battle, whether against interlopers, thieves, or weather. Always there was a tremendous payoff at the end of the road, whether that road was the Goodnight–Loving Trail or a simple path from sod to gate built from mesquite. At times, ranching is like that.

At times, there is loneliness—a sense that you are alone against the world. With this comes very real knowledge of vulnerability, usually hidden behind a veneer of machismo, marketable image of the silver screen. Ranching is called a battle sometimes. It feels that way when the end of the day brings yet another political attack, when the day was spent working on the land, doing everything in your power to make it better, failing as often as succeeding. Conservationists feel the same way when their muscles and hearts ache, so why is it that instead of sharing a common aim we rise to battle? In battle we fight with words our "opponents" don't understand; concepts they fear, hard lines in erosive soil. We hurt, and we give hurt back, despite the fact that we want the same thing in the end.

Ranching is an understanding—an acceptance that clouds bring many things: rain and snow, essential moisture to plants, fire and wind, and false hope. But clouds carry shade from the hot sun. And children on horses watch clouds, describe them, see wind miles over their heads, and grow from tiny horsemen to fighter pilots in an instant. In these clouds are small signals that tell bugs to hatch on water so that fish rise and let parents and children share pure joy. Clouds can carry frustration, and they can carry hope. Sometimes both come out of the same clouds.

The reality of ranching is manifest in the uncertainty of a new day, rain or dry wind, cattle happy or not, water plentiful or gone altogether. As much as the joys that come with a day that goes well, the hell of ranching is why people stay. It is a masochistic, roller coaster of a career choice perhaps, but the good days are so good that they fade realities to gray and illuminate the mind. Ranching is no place for pessimists; they will be rewarded daily until they have no greater horror to foretell. Stewardship is for optimists, those who see flames as dancers, new growth in the ashes of fire.

Therein lies a great oddity, paradox for a sphinx. In the public eye, ranchers are often portrayed as greedy, pessimistic, ready-for-battle warriors hell-bent on controlling their part of the planet. In their element—cracked hands immersed in snow-melt, patient hands massaging the uterine wall of a nervous first mother, soft hands on the head of a tired border collie, worn hands holding tiny hands—the same people don't quite measure up to that image. As we continually gain speed in society and communication, we seem to lose our ability to see into hearts and listen to minds. It takes patience and time to know people, and few seem to have either the time or inclination.

It doesn't help that ranchers are lousy communicators. They've been trained that way. For all of eternity, economics, politics, and sameness have defined their existence. They may have cussed the neighbors, but they were there in times of need. The average age of ranchers in the West is something like sixty-three years old; more have ridden in horse-drawn wagons than in airplanes. Today flocks of people fly to ranches to ride in wagons. A good percentage of ranchers lived through the Great Depression, fought in World War II or Korea, then stood in awe when their house had a telephone, even a party line. They came home from a war that made ranching profitable, then found themselves mired in an economy where nothing seemed to work. Inflation and intolerance rode the same horse, and the whole world went through an upheaval never before seen by modern man and woman.

The single most important meeting of the year was with the banker. Everyone who could borrowed money, just as ranchers borrow money now. We're talking lots of money, more money than most dot-coms need to start and operate for a couple of years. There were no investors, no markets for sharing risk. There were kids who worked for nothing, there were hands who wanted to be paid weekly even though calves were sold only once a year, and there were calves that weighed something and buyers who wanted them to weigh something else.

Merchants were gracious, but they kept their pencils sharp and looked at the bottom line. In a community, you paid your bills: you met your obligation to your neighbor, though you might speak quietly to the merchant at the high school football game, and ask for time—just a little more time—to pay for bolts and nuts and nails and wire. Nothing else carried the stress or importance of making ends meet. Kids learn from parents. They see stress, and the stress they see in ranching has a lot to do with money. The joy comes from the land.

"I miss the ranch," an elderly woman told me, and her eyes looked through me to snowy peaks and memories—frogs caught in bogs, fossils found on hillsides, boys kissed under trees while the river roared. Her voice trailed off, and I saw her mind wander briefly, until she turned and addressed me again, this time eyes clear and strong. "I don't miss the pressure," she said.

When a group of people talk, they speak of what is most important to them at the time, the thing that is on their mind. When you are losing money and losing the place you know as well as the birthmark on your daughter's leg, you tend to focus on money. The fact that society has seen this side of ranching foremost is sad, but it is the last piece of reality ranchers would wish to share. They've been trained to talk about money, business, and success, though. Survival is continued existence, and this means an extended line of credit, nothing more or less. It is a shame that most people, even in the West, don't interact with ranchers often. The greatest contact is usually hunting season, the same time ranchers are shipping cattle and dealing with bankers. Tensions are high, and time is ebbing for both hunter and rancher. Neither gets a clear picture of the other.

There is a hidden culture in ranching. Sadly, it is the intimacy people feel with land on which they live. Sadly, because this is truly the way most would choose to be seen and remembered, the gift they offer their children and grandchildren. Saddest of all because the greatest gift to society, perhaps, is a subject not spoken of, and in the void a cultural chasm is allowed to widen. Instead of showing pride in the habitat they provide, ranchers run silent and deep. There is true fear in knowing where certain mice live, where grizzly bears den, where black-footed ferrets roam, for soon an agent of government may come prowling.

Only when trust is absolute will most landowners share these pieces of their heart, then only in confidence, and more often than not with a certain sense of embarrassment. I've had plants brought to me in Styrofoam cups, cared and tended horseback for a full day, to see if they are rare. The phone rings at daylight with a description of a new bird at the feeder. We speak of deer, and grass, and water. For most, the health and vigor of their calves is an indicator of the health of the land, wild things, plants, and water. Many monitor other things as well. Fish as big as footballs are important, as are hatches of grouse. Big deer indicate an adequate number of small deer. Ducks on ponds and elk in meadows mean something. When my neighbors and I smile and kick dirt, these are the things of which we speak. Sometimes for hours. Sometimes for days.

When we talk of calf weights, percentage of cows bred, prices, and how much feed we have left, it is almost a competition to see who is worse off. Business news, really. How cattle do in our own backyard is a barometer—sometimes an indication of problems, sometimes confirmation that the year was really pretty good. The general public hears the discussion of calves, calculates the value, assumes wealth, and walks away.

In the advance of darkness, where ranchers let their breath out slowly, hang arms over pickup beds, and speak of deer and ducks, there are few witnesses. These are discussions rooted in uncertainty, fear, and vast knowledge. The talk bounces erratically, irrationally, emotionally. It is both friendship and competition, the things upon which communities are built. Fathers hand sons to neighbors they have cussed and embraced, so sons might learn from someone else, and not be ruined by fathers. In ranching culture, many young people find themselves by skipping generations. But family is formed by the land, that community of people who *know* Horse Creek, Lance Creek, or North Piney.

Intimacy with land is a cultural gift ranchers offer, but economic argument defines the image. When ranches sell and tears flow, salty water is ignorant of economic loss. Tears reflect loss of an intimate friend. This is the weight of stewardship.

I still walk to the very place I saw the first frog on this ranch, that place where the first salamander slid into the mud, the tree where young peregrines rest in wait of migration. I know ditches that seep, and those that cut, places once eroded and raw, now filled with silt and dense vegetation. I sit by holes where big fish hide and feed them grasshoppers.

My children have found places where warm water comes from under the land—places to swim, places ducks know in winter. Kids are cut from whole cloth, and they like to talk. They tell these stories to anyone who will listen. They bring notes home from school for talking too much.

The children are small. They still remember cattle—the Joe Cow, One Sixteen, Snake Horn, the Sweetheart Cow—and they remember wild things they see. Herons in the River Meadow. A sick deer in the brush behind the shop. Moose in the front yard. Rattlesnake on the porch. Lizards. In their eyes, these things go together. After all, in their youth they have seen most of the neighboring ranches turn into housing developments. They see these things more closely sometimes than the rest of society. Their bus that was nearly empty is now full. They see more dead rabbits on the well-traveled road—you can only outrun so many cars in a lifetime of rabbitry, it seems, or perhaps some people just don't watch for rabbits.

I am still a relatively young man. As such, I stand in awe of those the age of my father, men and women whose minds are sharp, memories intense, body and soul tied to the land on which they live. When my great-aunt was in her eighties, she lost her sight, and compensated by listening more clearly. She knew the day the bluebirds came home because she heard them. When she lost her hearing, she compensated by some other sense. When she told me there should be bluebirds at the window soon, I asked how she could possibly know such things. She said the day felt like bluebirds. A little less bite of snow on the breeze. Perhaps a bit of squish in the soil, a harbinger of frost coming out of the ground. Warmer sun on her face through the kitchen window. Mountain bluebirds danced at that window, busily checking crevices, gathering twigs, fluttering for her unseeing eyes, singing to her deaf ears. They were there. The bluebirds were *there*.

I have learned not to argue with these things. Instead, I have found that buried in the culture of ranching lie observations and passions for all things on the land, and we can learn from them, whether statistically significant or not. At the dawn of the information age—first predicted, now reality—we have potential access to more than we ever imagined. The risk lies in becoming so infatuated with what is new that we let go of what is real. Our history and our future are one and the same. The trick lies in listening and learning from whence we have begun.

Things move slowly in ranching. This is a remnant of seeing too many schemes and instant solutions, all of them inconsistent with the pace of the land, none of them as patient as the grass. There is no fast money in ranching, just good and bad years, and lots of years in between. Those must be the normal years they talk about on the weather report. There are lots of moving parts—weather, markets, help, old neighbors, new neighbors, inventory of living things that never quit eating, equipment, parts, the latest rage in technology, quick fixes, and things that have worked for nearly a century. Perhaps the culture of ranching is merely a matter of sorting priorities. On normal days, you chase your tail, and parts, and cows. On a good day you count deer in the meadow, beavers in the creek, and new birds on the feeder.

I manage a ranch owned by The Nature Conservancy. Red Canyon Ranch is a jumbled landscape on the southeastern flank of the Wind River Mountains in central Wyoming. Six rare plants live here, one of them found nowhere else on the planet. Most of the wild creatures native to the region are present. The plants have been here longer than any of us. There are interlopers; the creeks are filled with fish from Europe, and we battle weeds imported for ornamental enhancement as well as species brought here to enhance the economic potential of the land. Apples are grown in an orchard more than a century old. White-tailed deer have worked their way from the East into these creek bottoms. Lilacs bloom and break harsh winter wind and snow. I did not make this place. Like the bluebirds or mule deer I love, I can only claim to live here. My care is limited by my understanding of the system—of time—of plants and animals that speak only in life and death. In caring for the land, I must

try to hear silent calls for help, see invisible images of joy and pain, feel the immensity and nothingness of fog.

I am an advocate for wild creatures, rare plants, arrays of native vegetation, clean water, fish, stewardship of natural resources, and learning. I believe these things are compatible with ranching, sometimes lost without ranching. Some people call me a cowboy. A lot of good cowboys call me an environmentalist. I suppose there are lots of labels you can attach to me. There was a time when doing so was hurtful, so I threw back labels of my own. We throw a lot of anger at each other with words. It doesn't do much for the land, really.

As I wrote this essay, my oldest son read with some interest, and said nothing. A few days later we rode in the pickup, arms out the windows, dust in the mirror, red dirt caked on eyeballs, lips, and sticky necks. I finally asked him how he saw the culture of ranching, as eleven-year-olds see the world, and he offered a story that left me speechless.

"Did you know, Dad, that if you write the word 'red' in green and ask a small child to tell you the color, the answer will be 'green'? But if you show the same word to an adult, the answer will be 'red.' Children see the color, not the word. Adults see the word, and not the color."

In a complex world of ecological mystery, we cannot allow words and images to limit the opportunity to learn from one another. We must respect the places from which we gain understanding. The world cannot be framed in contrast of black and white, in pure scientific light. Ranchers live in a gray world where subtle hues of green and blue gleam as vividly as neon, where the color of a bird can make a month seem right, and yet there is no incentive to speak of the color of birds. The time has come for all of us who care about the natural world, as well as our own communities, to think beyond labels, stereotypes, and misconceptions. There is no room for the language of hate and intolerance to supersede conservation on the land. Between eagle and cottontail, polit-ical solutions mean nothing.

The time has come to see colors, not words.

SHADES OF GRAY

I am a child of the West. My blood runs neither red nor blue—it appears to me to be the pale green color of sagebrush. Seven species of sage are found where I live and work. Each smells different. Feels different. Red dust coats my hair, itself thinned by patches of gray. My border collie is black and pink. Smells of sage, sometimes skunk and decay. The hair nearest her body is white as snow. It snowed yesterday, soaked into the red soil, fed the sage, turned my children red. Pleased and nourished their souls. People take on the character of the land around them. Today the thermometer pushes seventy degrees. A chinook blows out of the north. Patches of gray appear on the landscape.

Patches of gray may best describe patterns of arid land ecology, of ranching, of life in this region. These patches are elegant and wonderful things. Subtle shades of gray define black sage, big sage, bitterbrush, and sumac. Blue-grays tint stands of wheatgrass more ancient than humankind. Green-gray paints Idaho fescue. Depth of color tells the story of organic matter on the ground. It differentiates species. Bright red is dogwood. Dark red, chokecherry. Coyote willow lies between this spectrum of reds. Other willows are yellow or white. Birch is black. Buffaloberry is silver-gray.

Lack of startling color is the whole world in the ecology of ranching. In the hair of deer and humans, feathers of birds, leaves of plants, shades of gray differentiate. In these plain patches lie secrets of rangeland ecology, essential links and pieces of the frame that teach us to revere, and suspect extremes, whether dark, light, or color. Greens are verdant only when heat and water come together in proper fashion— before snow is totally gone, before sun takes over. Like the brief dance of the sage grouse, plants in my landscape find little time for splendor. This is a good thing. For only when you learn to discern shades of gray can you truly appreciate the brilliance of a goldfinch.

The western landscape in which I work has a harsh and violent history. It is a landscape ripped from its roots, stood on end, blasted by lightning, washed by torrents of rain, waterlogged by snow, baked by drought, frozen by cold. For thousands of years this landscape has been grazed, burned, rested, desiccated, flooded, and washed. Rangeland ecosystems are immense and intensely complex. Mere strides take us from hard, cold desert to lush, dense riparian habitats. Sometimes we can travel for hundreds of miles in an apparent sea of nothing but sagebrush and grass. It is a vulnerable thing, this land, and it can be transformed from lush wellspring to barren waste. But this is incredibly resilient land, and the processes that shape it make it rich in diversity of life. It can be transformed from barren waste to lush wellspring, too, and sometimes we forget that.

Natural systems build themselves up and tear themselves apart. Aldo Leopold tried to teach us to understand systems: to see ourselves as part of a greater world. We can't control the natural world. But we can try to live within the variations it throws our way. The same waters that allow willows to grow rip beaver dams from streams. The same animals that devastate plants prepare a world in which plants may grow. Browsing by animals affects chemical composition in plants, which attracts insects, which provide the food base for many of the world's birds. These are not simple things. They are the elegance of life; we will never comprehend the magical realities that mesmerize and remind us that we are not in charge of the world.

People make choices both spatially and temporally. We choose to maintain species of rare plants knowing full well they are inconsistent with other natural values, and without knowing why they fit into the overall picture. We choose to maintain forests of pine as we lose aspen stands. We choose to convert rangeland to farmland and, after that, eliminate all biological choices for the land. We choose to manage for creatures and plants that rely upon things we do not understand. We have no idea whether some species are doomed by evolution or whether they are emerging and undeterred by our efforts on their behalf.

In landscapes where the single ecological truth is chaos and dynamic change, we seem obsessed with stability. Instead of relishing dynamic irregularities in nature, we absorb confusion and chaos into our own lives, then demand that natural systems be stable. We ask systems that evolved in geological time to respond and perform in our own lifetime. Instead of engaging right-brain ideas—and testing even the most hare-brained of them—we answer ideas with reasons why they will never work. We argue about math and dream little of process. We hide hatred in emotional debates about science. Science becomes political, evangelical, competing for limited dollars, pleasing masters of inquiry. Questions are built around dollars instead of ideas. Answers become churches of high divinity. Proof is in numbers, amalgamation of statistics, mathematical design, and, ultimately, interpretation of numbers. Every ecologist seems to have a separate take on what the numbers say. We are a fast-food society. We want answers now. If the answers are incorrect or incomplete, so be it. Ecological inquiry is relegated to courtrooms and political chambers for instant determination.

The fate of landscapes ultimately lies in the hands of people on the land. Are we really content with the notion that butterflies and bears will both do well in a landscape where they cannot compete? It seems incongruous, incomprehensible, that we would turn the fate of the land over to those who cannot hear snipe feathers slicing wind overhead, whose sense of feel is immune to frostbite in winter. Only when we strive to learn and share, rather than lecture and control, will we find our ability to care for land enhanced and expanded. We may even find our sense of touch. In doing so, we will find questions unanswered. But we will rejoice that we can pass them to others anxious to learn.

Rivers run. Soils wash. Grasses grow. Rarely do we speak of what we desire the land to provide. As a result, our measurement of progress is skewed at best.

Have we lost the vital connection between the questioner who lives on the land and the scientist who can analyze questions built on decades of observation? The person who watches a bright bluebird without counting the bird is blessed for life by the meeting. The person who counts birds without seeing their color does no more than move blue beads on an abacus. Those who see the bird, and drop their work to follow it, and fly with it in their dreams, will see the land from the keen eye of the bird.

Late in April 1999, nearly a quarter mile of rock face fell from the Red Canyon rim to the valley below. Six feet of snow combined with temperatures below zero—then into the upper seventies—cleaved tons of ancient ocean bed from its mooring above an eroded basin and tossed it aside as casually as a grizzly ladles spent salmon from a receding stream. Boulders larger than trophy homes bounced and tore forest from the earth, guided by nothing but gravity and terrain, luck of bounce, shape of fragments. Some boulders reshaped the creek below. Others left scars as large as coal mines on the face of the hillside. Laws prohibit such things, but they happen. Sometimes these little things should remind us we are not in charge of everything—including time, rain, and the wonderfully imperfect tilt of this planet in its irregular loop about the sun.

Landscapes of the West were shaped by plant–animal interactions, by fire, and by natural processes we are incapable of managing, or "manhandling." The level of herbivory was as varied as the landscapes themselves. In the Great Plains, there is little question that bison, elk, prairie dogs, and other mammals shaped the environment. We still see evidence of these species in wallows, trails, life, and vegetation that defines the region. In subarctic rangelands, caribou, moose, and hares drive systems physically and chemically. Big mammals, in systems devoid of cattle or sheep, with a full complement of native predators, influence plant chemistry, affecting insect preference, providing food for birds. They also have an impact on vegetation, one that we might not accept if the alterations were done by livestock.

In the northern Rockies, bison may not have been the keeper of the grassland, but other animals were equally integral to the web of life. The oldest dated art on rock reminds us that wild sheep, elk, deer, a complement of insects, disease, drought, fire, and erosion were essential to systems we try now to understand and control. Some landscapes evolved without large herds of animals. Some evolved with no large animals at all. Not all of these are arid lands. Some are lush systems where large grazers simply didn't have either presence or influence. There is a wide variation in landscapes, and a wild variation within landscapes. Without doubt, domestic livestock have had an influence on many of these. And some may never recover from the experience. Others may recover slowly, but it will not be ecological limitations that swing the balance. Instead, the reality of world economics may have a greater influence on many ecosystems than our current ability to understand land.

Ask children what the word "grazing" means, and their answers will rarely be the same. Most will get around to eating of grass in the end, though their paths may wander from goose to moose, grasshopper to sparrow. Ask an adult, and the answer will almost certainly involve cattle, sheep, or horses—and, depending on political opinion, the word will be shrouded in black or white with few shades of gray to stimulate the eye. Extending the point, some are now engaged in a debate over the simple word "rangeland," certain that it means cow or sheep. To me the word means openness, a sea of vegetation, a vastness found in native lands of the western reaches of this continent. It may seem odd that so many ranchers end up at the edge of oceans—unless you have sailed the pale green sea of sage and grass. There is a magnetic pull to the unseen: to living things beneath the surface. It is a curious wonder, never sated, a childish yearning to learn, a hard lesson that we are not nearly as smart as we think we are.

As we entered the twentieth century, the word "fire" was equally incendiary. In fact, fire was virtually removed from the landscape. In its absence, homes and other refinements that now limit our ability to replace this essential natural process were born. Now we wonder how we might be able to bring fire back—not as a symbol of process lost but as a real influence on landscapes. In 1988, much of our largest and oldest national park burned in savage fashion. While we convinced ourselves it was the right thing, the natural way of the world, we knew better. For eighty years we had extinguished fires from cigar, campfire, and lightning with the same zeal, until suddenly we were no match for fire. Patch burns gave way to massive, complex fires that would likely have not occurred with the same intensity or scale.

We've grown up with two notions—one learned from a cartoon bear with a pointed hat, the other saying "fight fire with fire." Now we find natural fire impossible to mimic in most settings. Grass and trees that used to burn regularly have accumulated for decades. Fuels that never existed are now abundant. Habitats once maintained by fire are altered and overrun. And when they burn, they don't burn with "natural" intensity. We know in our hearts that fire in springtime is symbolic more than natural, but it is "safe" and rarely burns up summer cabins. Perhaps it'll do. But lightning and dry grass marry on hot summer days, and human presence is naught but fuel to a real fire.

Full agencies were created to eliminate erosion—to halt this menace in the same manner we taught fire to behave. At the same time, lands created by erosion were jealously guarded as prime farmland, and we built levees and dams to protect these lands from change. Countless national parks and landmarks were created, monuments to erosion: Grand Canyon, Bryce Canyon, Badlands, Colorado National Monument, Zion. There are more, every one a spectacular example of

soil erosion running unchecked, even as we frown and allocate funds to control erosion upstream and downstream. We
admire on the one hand, we control on the other, even as we
know we are but one massive spring thaw, one torrential rain,
one earthquake or eruption away from what will be. Despite
our efforts, the Mississippi will one day spill itself into the
Atchafalaya Basin.

Like fire, erosion, and drought, grazing is a natural
process that can be stark and ugly. And, like fire, erosion, and
drought, grazing is essential to the maintenance of many natural systems in the West. Bison were an integral influence on
western ecosystems, but bison were not the only large herbivore
on the landscape. Elk were common from desert to mountain.
Wild sheep dominated enough of the landscape that Shoshones
were referred to as "sheepeaters" by other tribes. Caribou and
hares shaped the rangelands of the Arctic regions. And because
adults tend to overlook other grazing creatures, we forget the
impact of grasshoppers, rodents, birds, and other organisms
that have long shaped the West.

Only recently have we begun to understand the cyclical
nature of grasshopper outbreaks, though the devastation has
long been noted. Like many creatures of the arid West, these
rise and fall in response, not only to climatic conditions, but
their own voracity.

Grasshoppers require bare ground on south-facing
slopes to flourish. And when their eggs hatch, little grasshoppers create an environment for succeeding generations. Before

we fell in love with technology and sprays, grasshoppers may have defined the environment in a manner equal to the customary grazing animals named by adults. Late frost, heavy rain, and lush grass could contend with these insects that grazed the West—but these elements were not common. Grasshoppers were common.

Prairie dogs are now seen as an essential species in some western landscapes. In the absence of other grazing animals, they mow and remow grass, even pile it without eating. Prairie dogs even harvest shrubs, maybe to protect against predators. It has been theorized that the interaction between these small mammals and bison hinges on the ability of each to modify a world of grass that, in their absence, would burn. The interaction between prairie dogs, bison, and other grazing animals suggests that these species depend not only on one another but on extreme levels of herbivory some would decry as "overgrazing." Other species, burrowing owls, dung beetles, and many plants now rare, rely on the same interactions.

Some species now petitioned as threatened or endangered have a vital need for grazing animals. Species as common as the bluebird, as rare as the black-footed ferret, as unknown as the mountain plover, are tied to grazed lands. The edge between grazed riparian areas and lesser grazed sagebrush steppe may mean the difference in survival for species like sage grouse and swift fox. Mule deer require a world of brush and deciduous trees—both dependent on a regime of fire and grazing. These are not species endemic to the Great Plains. They evolved and flourished in the Rocky Mountain West. These creatures and plants thrive on chaos and confusion. They revel in the results of fire, herbivory, and open space.

If my blood runs sagebrush green, it manifests itself in passion for species that define my world. A mule deer makes my blood rush. Sage grouse, standing tall and strutting, booming, make me smile. Bluebirds most often return to this ranch on the day of my mother's birth, in a snowstorm, bringing light to a world that sorely needs illumination. There are other species, but they are not the message. Children who see color instead of words are the message.

If we hope to carry a full complement of biodiversity beyond our own meager time, we must begin to manage for chaos and confusion for the full range of successional states that allow birds to hide in tall grass and forage in open meadows. We have to think not of species, not of isolated populations of rarity, but of systems that allow these species to survive. Large landscapes offer not only large opportunity but a greater margin of error and a chance to learn about connections we simply cannot see. When I think of land, I remember the song of a meadowlark—in the dead of February winter—in a marketplace in Guadalajara, in a cage: a song as common as sunrise. Through metal mesh I stared at a bird that was hatched thousands of miles north, maybe even on the ranch where I work. We think too small. We have to learn to think and understand at levels we have never comprehended. Mathematics may explain that yellow-breasted bird in a Mexican

market, but numbers won't give it a place to live and repro-
duce. A ranch can offer that.

If we choose to allow future generations a chance to
make mistakes of their own, and correct some of ours, we must
think and work on scales uncomfortable to science. Last fall I
followed a peregrine falcon for the better part of a day—a young
male resplendent in slate overcoat and auburn cummerbund.
He rested in a juniper tree on private land, rose as if lifted until
he was airborne high above red cliffs, then rocketed down to
follow the creek bottom for two miles in a dive that made my
blood rush. Up in spirals, then hugging sagebrush as it followed
a mountain a mile west. In the space of minutes, he covered ten
sections of ground, some of it private, some federally owned,
some state. The night before, he left the place where he was
fledged, a canyon wall farther west, on Forest Service land. It is
through these eyes that we must learn to see.

If we wish to maintain intact systems, we must learn to
manage and inquire on a scale that recognizes biological lines
rather than lines of property ownership. What is best for the
landscape will only be realized when it can be accomplished in a
manner that follows the flight of the falcon. We cannot demand
fire, or rest, or surgical applications of grazing if we cannot sustain the link between wetland silt and its parent rock. The scale
on which we choose to think is critical. Choose too small, and
we could find ourselves managing fleas while forgetting the
dog. We cannot begin to reinstate fire on the scale of times past
without a base of forage upon which we can build alternatives.

The notion of grass-banking and swing allotments is the solid model for incorporation of natural process in an economic world shaken to its core. We may choose to use this approach to achieve rest, to rebuild precious riparian areas and wetlands, to restore fire in a natural sense. But it will require an approach that incorporates economic stability with ecosystem integrity. There are no quick answers.

There are only a handful of natural processes that humans can affect. Fire has been suppressed to such a degree that we now have conifers growing in areas that were once rich sources of winter forage, ensiled leaves of deciduous trees and shrubs. Grasslands and sagebrush steppe have become "stable states" of brush that now defy succession either forward or back. Where fire does occur, it is often with a vengeance born of decades of silence. And the result is not fire of the frequency and magnitude once necessary to maintain natural process on the landscape. Fed by years of suppression, fire is a furious storm that takes all in its path. Not long ago, fires in the same place would have left islands of brush and grass untouched, a patchwork of time sewn into a cloth of diversity.

Of the other natural processes we can affect, most are related to grazing animals. Resting the landscape may seem logical to humans in need of the same, but rest was never the norm. It was the exception. Animals used the landscape as conditions dictated. In springtime riparian areas and wetlands were flooded with herds of elk, bison, sheep, and other species seeking the essential nourishment that would allow them to give birth, make milk, breed, and find strength to move higher as the sun did the same. Predators might have moved some animals, but they were few.

Many predators we now revere made their real living not by chasing the strong across the landscape to prevent over-grazing but by eating things that died because they were old, or weak, or left behind. Grazing animals did not move in response to predation—they formed herds in response to predation. They moved when they were out of feed or water. Grazing animals do more than just eat plants. Their movement, individually or as herds, their resting sites, their defecation and urination—all are interactions between animals and plants. Different animals eat different things. The same animals eat different things on different days, driven by seasonality, weather, and plant phys-iology. Some animals break down plant material. Others gain from the remains. Excited animals churn the soil; contented animals may compact it. In the northern Rockies, freeze and thaw equalize both. In other landscapes, where freeze and thaw are not a regulator, native plants have found other means of survival and perpetuation. Grazing animals, whether bird, cow, or sheep, have interacted with plants that anchor sky to soil, rain to river. Even in areas now declared unsuited to livestock (sometimes rightly so), adaptations of plants are cause for ques-tion. If there is no history of grazing animals, why are plants so elegantly armored against herbivory?

Other living organisms are crucial, too, but often ignored in debates over ecosystem management. Some insects pollinate plants. Others incorporate dung into soil. Tiny mammals take organic matter beneath the surface and offer up soft, rich dirt in which seeds might grow. Birds seek the fleshy fruit of trees and shrubs, drop the seeds, and perpetuate the stand. Beavers cut down the stand, slow water, store eroded soil, and add woody debris to the stream. There is an intricate web of interaction we sometimes comprehend but dimly. In many cases, ecological systems have advanced to a point where sameness, not diversity, is reality. A forest without fire, grassland without grazing, may look lovely. But it may also be next to sterile for the full range of species that rely on a mosaic of habitat types.

In the past half century, humans have wittingly and unwittingly removed the natural effects of fire and grazing from much of the western landscape. At one time, removal of fire was supplanted by aggressive harvest of trees for lumber and pulp. The removal of grazing animals has been more subtle, but some of the effects may now be showing scars. To salvage ranges from overuse and overstocking, the number of animals was reduced—a logical and correct analysis of the "tragedy of the commons" in Europe. It didn't take long for people to see that western ranges could not sustain a cornucopian view of natural resource extraction, and in some areas the impact of unregulated grazing by livestock led to irreversible changes on the landscape. So if livestock numbers were to be reduced, it meant that somehow the rangelands of the West would have to be regulated.

By altering the behavior of animals—mainly by string-
ing wire—and altering people's behavior—by subdividing
management from a landscape scale to one of individual allotments cut from the whole—impacts became more focused.
Some portions of the landscape began to recover from abuse.
The notion that a reduction in numbers was equivalent to
good management became a virtual law of natural resource
management. Rest-rotation grazing was implemented. While
this fix worked in the immediate term, it did not completely
resolve problems, and economic margins got tighter. As the
land available for grazing, or fire, or rest got smaller, the notes
at the banks loomed larger.

Our greatest challenge in ecology, and in conservation,
will be our ability to think, study, fail, and learn at scales that
don't lend themselves to scientific tidiness. We are living Leopold's fear: his distrust of science. We have reduced natural
science to a level where simple process is more important than
systems. We keep asking the wrong questions. An answer may
be statistically correct but biologically wrong. Science is seen,
not as question and wonder, but as certainty spoken in code.

As a rancher, or land manager, I am an insatiable con-
sumer of science. Should I choose to know the heart rate of a
three-day-old calf, how to manage three or four acres with two
steers, or four, or eight, a library might be available. Should I
choose to know what happens to a stretch of water when a pre-
cise amount of cow dung is dumped from a bucket, there are
answers. If I want to know the DNA patterns of four cutthroat

trout that look the same, the information is available. But if I want to know how to manage cow, moose, or goose to give those trout an edge, there is damn little help.

Our understanding of systems ecology isn't limited by answers. It is limited by questions. Our ability to see the future through the eyes of the bird is limited by our demand for satisfaction here and now. If we really care about life as common as bluebunch wheatgrass, mysterious as wolverines, rare as black-footed ferret, we can only try to keep the systems they need intact. And intact systems are ranches—an integration of land ownership that has precluded irreversible habitat loss. To paraphrase Wes Jackson, a poorly managed ranch is far superior to land turned by the plow. To paraphrase an ardent environmentalist, a lousy ranch is a whole lot better than a really good subdivision.

BLUEBIRDS AND BLACK COWS

At one time I might have harbored illusions of owning a ranch. My father's father was raised out of rock and water, third generation on the same piece of land, near a town that bears our family name on Main Street. My mother's father came west in 1931, with wife and new daughter, a dream, and precious cash. He nurtured a ranch out of glacial till, boulder fields, and red hills that ran more clay than water when it rained. When I entered high school, both ranches were still in the family. By the time I was a sophomore, both ranches were in other hands. And though we never spoke of it much at the dinner table, we knew our parents could never go home again. From that point on, we didn't visit those places as often, then not at all. Mom and Dad still spoke of their roots, strangely in past tense, and when they did, their remembrances came down to two simple things: land and people.

Thirty years later, I point those places out to my children as we pass by. The kids look out the windows and say little. I too am quiet, for I know exactly what they are thinking. My wife, always quick with a smile, support, encouragement, and optimism, chokes on her own question: "Am I teaching my children to love something they can never have?"

The ranches and homes lost to my parents went away for different reasons. In one case, it was a matter of scale and poor decisions. Poor decisions aside, the ranch would never have sustained the single family that tried to make it work through the 1970s. It was sold to the neighbors for enough money to pay off the note at the bank, build a new house up the lane, and allow the neighbors to keep their kids on the ranch. Today, despite acquisitions made in the late 1960s and early 1970s, these expanding families face the same questions of scale a single family encountered three decades before.

The math of ranching is hard-core new math, made harder to figure when you always knew the home place as a ranch built out of six ranches. Three generations ago, one of our family ranches was split in half between brother and sister when parents died. Now half of the whole is only a piece of one ranch. Follow the math. Six ranches were established in the 1900s, became one in the 1940s, turned into two in the 1960s, part of one in the 1980s. They have fared well. Down the road, there is a place that went from eight ranches to one, then divided into four, and, ultimately, became more than a hundred parcels on the market. The parcels sold. The ranch disappeared. I used to hunt sage grouse there, stealing them from circling falcons. There is no room for any of us now, let alone the cows that dotted the flat for a brief time in spring and fall.

The fate of the other ranch is still unknown. My grandfather sold it to his sons, an early inheritance, more or less. In retrospect, it was an amazing choice: to leave a piece of ground he nurtured from nothing into something, at the age of fifty-five, to his own young sons. He knew their strengths and their weaknesses. Brothers fight sometimes. Suddenly a ranch that was home and profit to one family had to be home and profit to two families. A ranch that would buy a new truck for the price of five calves now had to buy two trucks, and new trucks were twelve calves each. Within a few years, a new pickup was twenty calves; nights in the calving barn were still twelve long hours. In the end, one brother became a judge, the other a Realtor and public relations specialist. They were good at what they did, and they were happier. After all of the hard times, sweat, and fret, they had a little money in the bank, a "stake," as the old cowboys said, and they made the most of it. The ranch was loved by a man who lived in the old family house and worked for a man who had lots of money and visited rarely. Not long after the ranch was sold, the new owner told the Realtor he would really like to have one more piece of ground he had seen, a really pretty place, with lots of aspen and grass.

"Buy it," he told the Realtor, who doubled as a brand inspector, confessor, card dealer, and rancher himself.

"It's yours," the multitalented Realtor smiled.

"Dandy," said the buyer. "Tell me how much to make the check for."

"I mean, it's yours already," the Realtor said. "But I guess you can write a check to yourself. My commission is seven percent."

Today that same ranch is the subject of daily rumor. One day it will be subdivided, sold to Japanese golfing aficionados, or lost to foreclosure. The land is now an appreciated asset, not a source of income. What are the choices for this portion of the ecosystem? It may be "saved" by some conservation organization, or by a caring soul who can afford to own land that doesn't produce the standard rate of return, a place that eats money for fixing fence, moving water, and paying taxes. More than likely, this ranch will become a series of houses, each with lane, horse, septic tank, well, and partial water right that is misunderstood. The houses will be nice, the wine old and red, the view spectacular, unless you saw it once as a place to raise twin fawns, or build a nest, or let out a deep, rasping croak that would attract a sleek, stylish, green mate. One rumor does not persist . . . the cows are gone . . . and no one would believe for a minute that a working ranch will reemerge from this dream.

Not long ago, agricultural lending was founded on the same premise, allowing debt to pile up, patient that markets would cycle as they always had, that there would be periods of gain and periods of loss, and that they would even out over time. Interest rates would sustain that ebb and flow, and while land sold back and forth it was priced according to its productive ability. As long as the value of the note was in line with the value of the land, it was a safe investment.

There was a cultural phenomenon buried within this economic world: a premise that some families would grow, others shrink, and that family business was a thing to be valued.

Access to land was fiscally possible because people built legacy at the same time that others retired. It was the same ebb and flow bankers saw in commodity markets. Values were consistent, and it was possible to build a place up, cash in and retire, and leave the new owner with a better piece of ground.

In the Sandhills of Nebraska, families have grown and declined for nearly two centuries. People there tell of working for an older couple, getting a chance to buy the place where they worked, raise a family, and see their own children sell it back to the great-grandchildren of the original owners. Now land values are driven higher than reasonable economic sense allows, and yet the ranches sell to ranchers. The buyers are people frustrated by lack of access to forage on public lands in the West, suddenly able to cash out the scenic value of their private lands one home at a time, and get the heck out of Dodge. Everything comes down to economics, and economics comes down to access to grass and water. For every permit reduced to economic uselessness, you can find a nearby riparian area converted to houses. For every millionaire made by selling the creek bottom to newcomers, there is a young person outbid in his own backyard. Perhaps it is just survival of the fittest, but it may be time to wonder if that ecological premise really fits the economic world. Maybe it fits Wall Street, but does it truly fit the Flint Hills of Kansas, shortgrass prairie of Colorado, or what is left of the Palouse prairie in Washington?

Sometimes, what is owned and what is known are far apart. In the world of Daniel Quinn's *Ishmael,* Leavers owned little and cared much for land that bound them together. Takers owned much but knew little about the land that was forced to sustain them. They never shared strawberries with a bear, fed grasshoppers to fish just to see them rise, or sat and looked at land without boundaries. If there wasn't enough cash in calves, there were plenty of dollars in the land. Just as long as it was flat enough to roll a golf ball, set a foundation, or see mountains from a picture window.

Ranches go through their own path of succession, just as plants occupy land. At one time land might have been land, but it was fought over as forcefully as dogs mark territory, bears claw trees, or eagles kill falcons. Native peoples fought for certain places that offered opportunity for survival—the greatest shelter, most food, best water. Right or wrong, these were the same lands snatched up as the nation grew. Color aside, people could easily pick out the best land. And when settlers came west, land was viewed in a pragmatic Jeffersonian light. Aridity defines these western landscapes, and those who would last would be those who held claim to water. Early homesteaders occupied creek bottoms and river valleys first and did what came naturally. They stuck a plow in the ground and farmed. In deep alluvium, farming worked, as it did on vast plains well watered by perennial rivers and streams. But many who came later dug the plow into lands that should never have felt such rough surgery. An early leader in the cattle industry, R. S. Van Tassell, said at the turn of the century, "I won't live to see the day, but many of you will, when people will regret that they ever plowed up this buffalo grass sod." In 1934 another ranching industry icon, Dugald Whitaker, said to his fellow ranchers, "We have lived to see that day."

Seven decades later, we continue to see the effects of these conversions, yet are unable to recognize the same progression in our own communities. Succession of a single ranch is driven by economic reality—by the fact that the note at the bank cares little for drought, disease, or decision. And like the newfound wealth in electronic marketplaces, *volume* is essential to the economic integrity of a ranch. A cowboy who can handle 50 cows can handle 500; the pay's the same. When volume is limited by access to forage—whether on federal land that is regulated or on private land priced out of reality—time is the only factor remaining. When cows grazing native plants are no longer a viable option, maximizing output per acre leads to farming. And when farming is rendered inefficient by loss of soil, or markets, or cost of inputs, houses replace cornstalks up and down alluvial valleys once known as riparian areas.

In the succession of ranching, lands once grazed were plowed in order to extract a greater return per acre. Native plants and animals were now found in secondary states of succession, often blasted by herbicides to keep them in check. Pheasants did really well. Bluebirds met unbridled hell. When the concept of higher returns per acre failed, it was the result of people in pastoral economies being reduced to poor farmers on poorer land. The farms grew smaller as pieces were sold off in reverse of their productive capacity for hobby farms and homesites. This process, too, is an intricate web of life and death, a response to economic and social pressures that has a massive effect on biological diversity and even ecological potential. At its earliest roots, the business of ranching was perhaps one of the simplest mimics of natural process in the history of human civilization.

None other than Aldo Leopold made it clear that mandating a land ethic would fail. His admonition that the prayers and resolutions of the public would do naught ended with a simple statement: "All the non-farming public can do is to provide information and build incentives on which farmers may act." This notion is particularly salient today. My friend Gregg Simonds calls it "rational behavior," the sane reaction of people to economic signals they receive. Right now, the main economic signals ranchers receive relate to domestic animals and hay. Many if not most ranchers would be happy to raise wild sheep, bluebirds, mountain plovers, or frogs instead of cattle, but markets for wild creatures are almost solely consumptive, not at all unlike markets for Abbey's "stinking, bawling cows" or Muir's "hooved locusts." Markets for livestock are pretty simple. Two or three companies process all the calves raised throughout the country, and when they want to pay for cattle, the guy who raises calves and plovers gets more money. When they want to not pay, the guy on the land receives not.

Markets for wild things aren't a whole lot different. If the wild thing you feed and sustain grows horns, or swims and fights like heck on three-weight line, or flies straight enough to be blasted with scattered shot, you may become economically viable, sustainable, even visionary. But these markets exclude a portion of society from access to resources the public owns, and they offer little or nothing to species less desirable on the den wall. That may be just as well; women's hats and men's watch fobs contributed mightily to the extinction of the Carolina parakeet and ivory-billed woodpecker.

Economic signals for plant and wildlife conservation are perhaps just as logical and convoluted as cattle markets. In Texas, great big white-tailed deer are a cash crop, bigger than the beef market for some. Warblers and vireos, though far more important to the web of life in ranching landscapes, are viewed by some as a nuisance to development. White-tailed deer are under no pressure to survive and might in fact qualify as "pests" in a strict reading of the law. The standard line encourages ranchers to look for ways to capture the economic values of wildlife habitat, and these lines are becoming as flawed as a monopolistic cattle market. In the sagebrush behind my house, there are lots of potential dollars in elk and mule deer. But there is nothing in the marketplace that tells me to leave grass for grouse, brush for song sparrows, or willows for flycatchers.

Therein lies a tenuous ground between what is ethical and what is economical. Many have chosen to forgo the money and maintain the spirit of community, but this posture will not last in the face of economic pressure. The time has come to develop markets that reward stewardship, not in the traditional image of cost-share, subsidy, or bailout, but in a framework where raising vireos and warblers is honorable and necessary. The lands of the

West are interconnected into a myriad of ecosystems. Loss of single pieces is an immense threat not only to species, but more importantly to process on a landscape scale. There will be people on the land. If these people are ranchers, they will likely be willing to forgo wealth. These are the stewards who offer opportunity at the species level, at the landscape and natural process scale, but only if we develop a marketplace that captures value in nature in the same manner ranchers sustain a business with cattle or sheep. It is not a question of which will win out. It is, instead, a matter of placing economics on a par with our intellectual and emotional value system. In a world of untold wealth in stocks, dot-coms, and other ventures, ranching remains a passion, a grossly illogical pursuit where millions in capitalized value return mere pennies on the dollar. The work is hard, the line between sustainability and failure razor sharp. There are still people willing to accept this responsibility, though they may be highly irrational. But so too are mice, and native fishes, and birds that sing sweetest when free to fly.

GIFTS FROM OLD COWBOYS

Two things fit me well.

One is an old, brown saddle made for my mother's father, the first year after they bought a ranch at Dubois, Wyoming, in 1931. My grandmother measured him as if she was buying him a suit, then fretted when the saddle failed to arrive by the appointed hour. She knew it was at the post office because she had peeked at it through the frosty windows. The postmaster understood the importance of the saddle, and plotted to open the doors at midnight, Christmas Eve, so she could claim it after church and surprise him in the morning. My grandfather rode the saddle for forty years. It was given to me when he no longer worked cattle, and I was learning the trade.

The other thing that fits me well is an ancient fly rod. Crafted of bamboo, the fly rod is a survivor of thirty years on the Big Piney Roundup. The eyes are tarnished, and most of the original wrappings have been replaced with household thread, whatever color was handy at the time. The cork handle is pockmarked from flies pulled free. Still, the fly rod is balanced perfectly, and will direct line beneath a willow bush like a dart. It came from my dad's dad, when he quit fishing and died.

Gifts from old cowboys, both were functional at once.

"You'll be needing one of these," each man said, as if he were handing me a lunch, or a pair of gloves.

Even as an idiot kid, I knew there was more to the saddle and fly rod than function. Old cowboys are like old coyotes; they don't get old by being dumb.

Saddle and fly rod were passage to time for thinking, and contemplation, at the very moment that a young man needed to sort things out in his head. Cowboys think best in the saddle, away from chatter and noise. Fishermen concentrate on the water before them, but their minds are miles away. Cowboys and fishermen are much more the same than different.

Catch a cowboy emerging from the winter, or off a long ride, and his mind will be overflowing with questions and answers. Often, the questions and answers fail to match perfectly, but there is great thought behind them, and if wisdom from horseback was only applied, things would work better.

When darkness forces the fisherman from the river, his first words will invariably be, "You know, I've been thinking . . ." In many ways, thinking is dreaming, but the fisherman has been sorting much more than the perfect pattern for the water that day. The dreams of fishermen are characteristically clear, if only at the moment they leave the water.

These gifts held purpose immediately, but as intended, both saddle and fly rod were more. Today, my oldest son casts an ancient fly rod from his great-grandfather. His brother rides in the saddle of his other great-grandfather. Blood runs thicker than water. Heritage is intact. Both have a sense of themselves, put in context by a sense of their past, something they can touch and feel.

These gifts from old cowboys were a piece of themselves, a vital component of their very soul, things they valued most in life. For one, time spent horseback was his time, a chance to sort cattle and his thoughts. The other spent most of his days horseback, and his thinking time came at daybreak and nightfall, when cutthroats would rise to a perfectly placed fly.

I look at these things sometimes and wonder at the treasures I missed. For, in all of the leather and softwood that remain, the real gift from old cowboys was humanity. These were men who carved a life from nothing, made mistakes, and never lost hope. When they handed me their past, they provided a bridge to the future. Saddle and fly rod were never meant for me to use—they were meant to go to someone else.

Each of my children killed their first deer with the same rifle I used to kill my first deer. This is the same rifle my grandfather used to kill his first deer. My father used it as well. It is an original Winchester lever-action .25-.35, given to my great-grandmother because it was a smaller caliber, and didn't kick so much as a .30-.30. She carried it to the chicken house to blast bobcats, coyotes, and weasels.

This is the West we know. People are important here. Hand-me-downs aren't a sign of poverty. They are a measure of pride, and heritage.

Miles apart, we borrow sugar from the neighbors, but borrow enough so that we can bake *two* pies, and return the sugar in its proper form.

We are cousins, twice removed, yet as close as brother and sister. We take in stray dogs, barn cats, errant goats, and more than our share of people who need attention. We stop on the road to help others. We try to relate.

We do that because we usually do relate. Somewhere, we have a connection; we were stranded in a gulch, or dated a girl, or worked with a boy, or had a cousin that married someone. There is always a connection, and we seek that commonality because we live in a land with few people, and incredibly long streets.

We learn people through the land, and land through people. We draw maps of our homes on bar napkins, and we trade our livelihood by telephone. We clip good news of one another and send it around, so that those in the news don't have to brag. We flirt with old ladies, and we humor old men. We gather babies and snuggle them beneath our chins, then pass them on. We shake hands, and we hug one another. We take the children of friends and let them grow into themselves.

And so, when policies of government are rationalized with the admonition that they will affect only 2 percent of the people in the land, we tend to panic, and we get angry, and we worry for those who may be among the 2 percent. In the West, we know them.

We ride their saddles.

We fish with their fly rods.

McCHESNEY BIT

My grandfather's saddle came with one additional piece of tack, an old, rusted bit that had hung over the horn for twenty years without use. The bit was attached to a bridle once made of leather, now the consistency of tree bark, and made no real impression on me at the time.

"It needs cleaned up," my grandfather said in his classically understated manner. "But, it's a great bit, easy enough to use all day, and deep enough to get a horse's attention if you need to. It's a McChesney."

I thought no more of it, but found another headstall and put the pieces together, then hung it back over the horn and forgot I even had the thing.

"What's that bit?" Joe Budd asked when he saw it.

"It needs cleaned up," I said.

"I'd say," he agreed. "That's a McChesney."

I took the bit to my cabin and tried to clean up the rust. Gasoline did nothing much to help, and saddle soap was no better. In working on the metal, I found a pattern of metalwork running the full length of the shanks, but it was hard to tell exactly what the design might be.

I walked over to the main house and begged some silver polish from Ruth, and went back at the bit in earnest. The little cabin smelled like gasoline, lanolin, metal, and woodsmoke, but the rust and grime slowly gave way to the rag.

The bit was made of hardened steel, balanced perfectly. The shanks were long and elegant, clearly designed in the shape of a woman's leg. The port was set higher than most bits, at an angle that fit the mouth of a horse without bother, unless leverage was applied. Even then, the balance was such that the bit couldn't hurt much. It was, as Joe said, "an attention getter."

The polish and elbow grease made it more so. Silver inlay framed the rings where the headstall attached, and below the rings, an elegant, solid silver owl came to life. Beneath the owl ran a series of four engraved silver leaves, all divided by a long copper snake. On the inside of the shank was a single stamped word, "McChesney."

"It's probably worth more than your horse," Joe said from the doorway.

"I'd believe that," I said. My horse was one of Joe's old mounts, the last one to buck him off, and presumably, the next one to buck me off.

"I'm not sure I'd use that," the boss said. "They don't make bits like that one anymore."

Indeed they did not. J. R. McChesney was a Texas blacksmith who started out making bits and spurs out of harrow teeth. The shape of the pieces, the "gal leg" was a McChesney signature, and at one time, his company occupied a full city block in Paul's Valley, Oklahoma. All his work was high-quality, ornate, and designed for use by real cowboys. I could see differences in the etching of the leaves and the owls—different grip, different angle—each done by hand.

I talked to my grandfather about this matter, telling him I had cleaned the bit up, and looked into its heritage, and had second thoughts about using it every day. I even offered to send it back.

"I am not the curator of a museum," he said. "I do not have a museum in my house, and if I wanted a museum to have it, I would have given it to a museum. I gave it to you because you are the cowboy in the family now, and it's a damn good bit. If you aren't going to use it, then give it to someone who will."

That concluded one of our longer conversations, and for the next eight years, I polished the owls, leaves, and snakes, and horse spit polished the bit. When I left the ranch, the McChesney bit went with me, draped over the horn of my old saddle, tossed into pickups and car trunks, slid into and out of the mouths of horses in all twenty-three Wyoming counties. Invariably, someone would ask about the bit, and an old-timer would answer for me.

"That's a McChesney," they would say, and that would be that.

"It was a classic," Doc Palen said.

We were standing in his basement, surrounded by hundreds of bits, spurs, saddles, chaps, photos, and other western memorabilia. Doc had dedicated his life to caring for animals, their owners, a family, and the heritage of western art, from pencil sketches to silver inlay. He was in the process of donating most of it to the local museum, and he pulled out a McChesney, almost unused, and asked if it was the same. I nodded.

Doc said the bit was probably made in the late 1920s, or even a couple years after McChesney died in 1928. The name was stamped into the shank, which made it a later version but even that put it nearly fifty years old.

I told him about my grandfather's curt reply to my suggestion that it shouldn't be used, and Doc laughed.

"You won't wear a McChesney out," he grinned. "Just don't lose it. You'll never get it back."

In 1993, I weighed the merits and downsides of managing a ranch for one of the world's largest conservation organizations, a move I felt would help build bridges between diverse interests traditionally at each other's throats. One rancher said at the time the bridge built would be over the River Styx, not an overly welcoming image.

My grandfather's health was failing fast, and he wasn't his usual self when I called for his counsel. Normally, his idea of conversation was direct, blunt, and staccato, punctuated by brevity. This time, he talked at length, told me about his move to the ranch at Dubois, how everyone in his family told him he was nuts, how it was the best thing he ever did. It was a place to raise a family, to find out what you were really made of, and a chance to follow your dreams.

"You go do that job," he said. "You'll catch hell, and you'll lose some friends over it, but you go do it. Nobody else will."

I tried to reason things out with him, play a little devil's advocate, like we always had, but it was his turn to talk. He chattered like I had never heard him speak. He talked about ranching, and marriage, and children. He had thoughts on government, the environment, friends, the law, and the sea, which I could hear behind him. Absent grass, there is nothing a rancher seems drawn to so much as the ocean.

"Take the damn job," he said. "You need to use that saddle, and teach one of those kids to use it. You're the last cowboy on my side of the family."

I took the job, and on the day I moved to the ranch, he died.

The "job" was managing Red Canyon Ranch, a rather bold move by The Nature Conservancy to operate a ranch in a manner that was both economically and ecologically sound. At the time, the notion was highly debatable, despite more than a century of compatibility between the two. Still, it was a chance to try out new ideas, to fail, to evaluate the relationships between dollar and the dirt. It was a perfect union of truth in the face of myth, and a challenge like nothing I had ever met before.

My grandfather, one of my most valued mentors, was dead. My friends were 300 miles away. My children were playing on a mound of toxic waste. My wife found that the kitchen sink drained below the floorboards of the house. She also found a raccoon on the kitchen sink. When she found a coyote on the front porch, she unloaded six shots from a .357 Magnum into its mangy hide, hitting it four times and rendering the hide totally useless. When I mentioned the hide, she reloaded the pistol. I suggested the hide was probably no good anyway.

I caught pneumonia and some other stuff (local medical terminology) and spent a couple weeks in intensive care. We bought a few horses, picked up a dog or two, discovered more than fifty feral cats in the attic, and made it through the winter. Spring brought rain, and red mud, to the degree that people knew my wife immediately from the dirt on her shoes. Some said hello. Some said nothing.

In the month of May, we rebuilt every mile of fence on the ranch. In June, we tore out twenty miles of fence. We dug ditches and moved water, and built more fences. And every day, we rode. Some days we rode to find out where the cattle were. Some days we rode to find out where we were. By July, the crew was dog-tired, and still we rode.

On July 10, we gathered the Barrett Slope and moved 600 cows and their calves to the mountain. The pasture was more than 5 square miles, rising as much as 1,000 feet from the bottoms of canyons and gullies to the ridges and crags at the top. Across the landscape, pockets of sagebrush, aspen, and dark timber were scattered like a bag of nails thrown from a speeding truck. It was the toughest gather on the ranch.

Jerry Bigelow had ridden every day for a month. Jerry was an intern who came from a stint in the navy, and he had a dream to be either a range manager or a chef (he chose chef). He asked for a top mount, and he deserved as much, so I gave him my favorite.

Topper was a big, catty gelding, the kind of horse that would fool you if you fell asleep. He was half Morgan, half quarter, smooth to ride, even tempered, and bulletproof. He was cat-quick around a cow, the kind of horse Harry Day said could "put a cow down a dog hole." He was the half brother of a pair I'd bought from Ed Fryer, a true horseman, and both were utterly spectacular.

When I bought him, Ed said there were only a couple things about the horse that made him imperfect.

"He has a game you play to catch him," Ed said, "and you have to get up and get on him, because he'll leave without you."

The other thing?

"You have got to get the right bit in his mouth," he said. "You put too harsh a bit on him, and he will fight you all day long."

I showed him the McChesney, and he smiled.

"I thought I was the only guy who used one of those," he laughed. "That'll damn sure do."

So Jerry rode Topper, raving all day about finally having a good horse, and doing the best job he'd ever done horseback. The day came off cool, the cattle were ready to move, and the calves were big enough to keep up. The sound of cattle attracted cattle, and some of the little bunches hidden out in the aspens and timber ran to catch up with the rest of the herd. When we reached the gate at the top of Tunnel Hill, the cows licked their calves, dropped their heads, and slowly wandered down the slope, paired up and happy. We were done early, headed back to the trailer, down to the ranch, back to food and beer. We slipped bits out and replaced them with halters, loosened cinches, and savored the day.

Lynn and the kids brought a cooler of cold beer to the barn, and we unsaddled, taking time to brush the horses out more than usual. Todd grabbed a hose, and another, and another, and he and the kids pulled it over to where we could cool the horses down.

"Thanks for the horse, Captain," Jerry said, and he offered his hand.

"You deserved it," I smiled. "You got my bit?"

The look on his face answered the question.

Jerry left with no beer, a flashlight, and a four-wheeler. I finally retrieved him an hour or two later, walking the road in the dark, fifty yards at a time, one side and then the other. He'd made about two miles.

"I put it on the fender," he said. "I knew to put it in the truck, and I forgot. I'm so sorry. It's not there. It's not there."

"We'll find it," I said, but I knew that would never happen. The only chance was that one of the neighbors, Old Jim, had found it while he was cutting poles and firewood. Jimmy had been driving in and out of the pasture every day, and he had to drive right past the place where we parked the trailer. He'd been up there on the same day, and he might have found the McChesney.

I called Jimmy and asked him about the bit, but he said he hadn't seen nothing.

"It was my grandfather's bit," I told him, but that didn't seem to change the fact that he hadn't seen a thing.

"If you find it, please let me know," I said, and I knew in my heart and soul that he had the McChesney.

This would be a test of me.

The theories around the ranch ran amok. Jerry left the conversation when we talked about the bit, but he looked for it almost every weekend. Some of the others suggested we should get the law involved. I'd already asked some of the local law, and they went into contortions about how the family in question was suspected of nearly every heinous crime in the county.

I was told they were poachers, group hunters, cattle thieves, water thieves, and the kind of folks that would steal the wheels off your truck if you left it parked in the wrong place. They were every kind of bad, according to some of the local gossip.

"How come nobody ever throws them in jail?" I finally asked the deputy sheriff.

"Well," he smiled slowly, "because they don't break the law, or if they do, they don't get caught."

In fact, for all the tales about the family's loose ties with
the law, they had been checked out repeatedly for poaching,
 and never once failed
to have the required
licenses, conservation
stamps, or permission.
They lived on deer and
elk for the most part,
but they lived on deer
and elk they harvested
legally. They didn't turn
out more cattle than
they were allowed on
federal lands, and when
they were told to bring
their cattle home, they
brought them home. They paid for everything with cash, and
they borrowed nothing. They worked from early morning
until late at night, and they never once asked for charity.

In September, I found a stray pair and a bull in the
meadow below Foster Draw. They didn't have an earmark, and
the ear tags were no help. The cattle were pretty skittish, but I
managed to get a look at the brand on the bull. I pushed them
down the canyon to the corrals, and when they wore down a
little, the cow and calf had the same brand. They were Jimmy's.

I had two choices. I could call Jimmy and tell him they
were there, or I could load them up and haul them home. I

chose the latter. I knew he didn't have much use for the owners of the ranch, but I figured it was a chance to meet him on his own turf.

Jimmy eyed me suspiciously when I drove into the narrow yard, then pointed behind me at a loading pen. He never left the porch while I backed in, and I opened the gate and let the cattle out. He hollered thanks and went back inside.

A week later, Jimmy called and told me he was still out two pair. One was a red cow with a black calf. The other was an old Hereford cow with a baldy calf. Had I seen them?

I had not, but I would keep an eye out.

Oh, and there was one other thing. The family had always hunted elk up above the ranch. They used to unload at the ranch and ride up from the corrals, but for the last few years, they hadn't been able to do it that way. He wondered if that might be alright?

"You bet," I said. "You can park in the yard, and if you need them, you can use the corrals."

There was silence on the other end of the line.

"There's a lot of us," Jimmy warned me.

"It's a big yard, Jim," I said. "Just leave the keys in the trucks, and if I need to move them, I will."

On opening day of elk season, I heard the truck coming, an old Ford stock truck laboring up the road, filled with horses and hunters. Daylight was an hour away, and a pickup and trailer were a quarter mile behind. Right behind that was another pickup filled with riders and saddles and guns, and behind that, another, and another. Three generations of family erupted from the machines, and a flurry of horses and humans spilled across the yard like a rodeo with no rules. I could understand the suspicion of some, and yet, I admired the dedication of the family before me.

I wandered out of the house and met Jimmy under the yard light. He grinned, not a single tooth in his head, but a head that had made a living on a little piece of ground for more than six decades. A slight breeze was blowing out of the West, and there was fresh snow on the ground.

"Good day for hunting," I said, and Jimmy nodded.

"My grandson found something the other day," he said, and he signaled a young man forward. "Thought you'd want it back."

It was the McChesney bit.

EARS FORWARD

For several years, my office was a converted slaughterhouse, a building once at the apex of processing locally grown beef, pork, and lamb. In its prime, the little frame building had been the most modern and efficient of the age. There were long tables for cutting and wrapping meat, cutting blocks, and a concrete floor that sloped to take blood and water through a set of drains. Outside the building, a system of clay pipes took the sludge to the hog pens down the hill. Not one drop of protein was wasted.

In the front corner of the building, a massive smokehouse stood as a sort of religious steeple to meats. Outside was a concrete pad for the woodstove, with a vent that funneled smoke into a two-story chamber where hams and sides could be hung until cured. It was an incredible construct; old-timers said the Greenough operation would process dozens of animals in a day. Even now, the hind quarter of a hog remains on a hook near the top of the steeple.

Inside that historic office, I was trying to balance out-of-control land prices with a tanked cattle market, buildings that hadn't seen paint or repairs for half a century, and a hay contract that sounded good to the farmer when it was signed, but suddenly seemed to evaporate in light of the drought. That was nothing compared to my charge to manage a five-year-old daughter who was hard-headed, inquisitive as a cat, and faster than an antelope.

She was gone again, but this time I could see her out the window, standing on the top rail of the corral fence on one leg, talking to a bay horse. The bay said nothing, but showed an obvious interest in this three-foot tall jabberbox. Maggie walked along the rail as calmly as if she were on an escalator, jumping from pole to post, then down again, until she climbed off the fence and poked her head through the bottom rails. The girl talked constantly. The bay horse said nothing, but his ears poked forward, and he moved a step closer.

Maggie walked out of sight, and then reappeared. This time, she had a hunk of hay under her left arm, held tightly by the fibers of her pink sweater, and she ascended the fence, right arm climbing, hooked over the rail, and then her feet, and again, until she was at the top of the fence. The bay was intrigued, and nodded his head, and the girl talked, and the bay horse took a step closer, and the girl talked and held the hay under her left arm, just above the red skirt her grandma sent her for Easter. The bay horse nickered and nodded, and came to the girl to eat the hay and have his ears rubbed.

This was communication, perhaps at its finest, and it was mesmerizing. The girl spoke a lot, but spoke no horse. The horse spoke no girl, but communicated just the same. For an hour they worked out an arrangement where the girl fetched and held hay, and the horse ate it, until the quick girl slid off the fence and onto the horse's neck, down to his back, whereupon she sat in complete control of the world. The bay continued to say nothing, but fully fed, rested beneath the chattering girl, equally in control of the world.

No matter how hard we try to communicate, if either of us is either incapable of hearing, or unwilling to listen, we will never connect. Our most powerful communication tool is our ears. Sometimes, all the ears need to do is point forward.

OTTERS DANCE

T he worst drought in the recorded history of Wyoming
began with five feet of wet snow, on the 20th day of April
1998, when twenty cows calved somewhere in the night, and
deer huddled beneath the red rocks until they were suffocated
by the crushing weight of the white water. An open winter had
let frost creep deep into the soil, which was as hard as the forehead of a bull. Behind the snow, a massive high-pressure system
warmed the landscape, and within three days, sixty inches of
snow melted and ripped anything unfrozen downhill, downstream, and gone. The red clay road never became muddy,
because the snow served as insulation, then turned to water
and vanished as effectively as flushing a toilet. For the next two
years, the total combined rainfall was less than what that one
storm dropped on the ranch. Over the next five years, less rain
fell than the average for a single year.

Those rains that came were isolated, intense, and worth
little. Some covered no more than a few acres, pounding so hard
that the rain raised dust, then vanished. In their wake came
bizarre rainbows of dirt and water, all of which disappeared
in seconds, leaving only the dusty haze. The baseball field was
especially prone to deluges and lightning, and on a short June

night, my oldest son, Joe, and I left a cloudburst in town, in a game he was pitching masterfully and winning, only to find ourselves bone dry and baking in the late-day heat on the dirt road that led to the ranch. The truck was air-conditioned, but our windows were open, and we watched the stream along the way, looking for beaver, muskrats, and fish feeding. It was a ritual. In the mornings, we watched the rim for bobcats, mule deer, and mountain lions. At night, we watched the bottom for creatures that emerged in the dusk.

In the grips of drought, the creek was something to cling to, a ray of hope, a reminder that this dry spell was not the end of the world, or even our own view of the world. It was also a reminder that mountains ultimately have nowhere to go but down, and rivers have little choice but to help them get there.

Joe was quiet, one of many alter-egos for a man of fourteen. There were things on his mind, I knew, but few would come out now. He had great heart, and tremendous strength, but he was small, and that was the only thing some people could see. Tonight, he had become large. His fastball snapped, and his change-up was merciless. Even the occasional knuckleball seemed ordained to find the strike zone. He was in meticulous control, and then the rain came, the game was no decision, and he was small again. I agonized with him, for I had been in the same hard place, many years before, and the memory still stung. I applauded his pitching again, and told him we all emerge differently, like butterflies.

"I am not a butterfly," he growled.

"Bad example," I agreed. "I'm just trying to help."

"Holy shit!" Joe yelled.

I could have thought this was a breakthrough moment, reprimanded him for his language, or continued with the lecture, but I was following the line of his arm and staring at the creek.

"Ho-lee shit," I muttered.

On the far side of the creek, no more than fifty yards out, five river otters ran with an easy, incredible grace. They flowed like a watercolor masterpiece, and the world became fine art, as if bronzes had suddenly awakened as acrobats. Adults in front and rear, three young in the middle, the otters undulated upstream as the creek rippled down. Pastel willows swayed in the breeze. The otters stopped, then dipped into the water and emerged on the near side of the creek. Translucent grasses hid them momentarily, and then they burst from the streamside into the open. Water droplets flew like crystal from their oily backs, and they danced in our eyes and our minds. Within moments, the otters darted back into the creek and disappeared.

They were utterly magnificent.

"Otters!" Joe grinned. "Oh, my God, Dad. Otters!"

In that instant, all life ended and began again. A sullen child became an anxious young man, life rekindled in his mind, flakes of gold sparkling against the green of his eyes. The entire moment couldn't have lasted more than three minutes, but the image remains crystalline. In fact, only three things remain clear memories of that year. It was mercilessly hot and dry. The calves averaged more than 600 pounds apiece for the first time, and on one June night, five river otters danced up Red Canyon Creek.

For both of us, the significance was visceral. Very few creatures are as stimulating as those at play, and none play with the grace and charm of otters. Their grandeur lies not in enormity, but in elegance and efficiency. As they moved, their grace seemed to interpret the rhythm of the stream, to enhance the melody of water swirling over stone. The whole valley took on new meaning and excitement.

Aside from the sheer joy they provided, the otters offered something greater. For a decade, my work had revolved around enhancing ecological values on the ranch, while at the same time generating an economic return. As soon as we seemed to find harmony with both, drought began to take a toll on the economy, and perhaps more. Now, the premier indicator of stream system integrity, a rare and elusive top predator, was living and propagating in the heart of the ranch. Their presence signified many things—water quality, abundant fish and other food sources, adequate cover, and lots of room for otters to dance unhindered. They were validation of a team effort, and cause for celebration.

Over the summer, the otters entertained many. A stranger in the grocery store showed me his grainy, distant photos of the otters at Deep Creek. One of the road crew asked me to verify what he had seen at the bridge over the river. Fishermen reported every set of fish bones left on the bank of the stream, and each track in the narrow margin of mud by the creek was cause to check it out (most belonged to beavers or raccoons, but many were otters). Suddenly, there was a bit of magic in our lives, something we could share in spite of the drought.

I wonder often what that moment was worth.

The hay we lost because of drought was worth about $25,000. The braces on Joe's teeth were worth $5,000, and his mail-order Nokona baseball glove was worth $175, most of which he saved on his own. The camera that took the digital image of the otters was worth $400. The calves were worth more than $700 each, an astronomical value for cattle. The cost to dust-guard the road was something on the order of $30,000. A gallon of diesel fuel cost a $1.45. But, exactly how much is a family of river otters worth?

In my brief tenure on that same stretch of dusty road, there were countless other moments. Bobcat kittens sitting on the red rim were cause for three children to be an hour late for school. A rattlesnake halted a troop of adults, until ten-year-old Maggie chased it away with a stick. Two varieties of orioles, three varieties of grosbeaks, and a willow flycatcher were life experiences for a mother and daughter from Rock Springs. A bear weaned her cub in the corral, and he sat and whined at the kids when they walked to the bus in the morning. The rest of the day, he ate a lot of earthworms, and whined at adults. Down at the mailbox, a savvy sage-grouse hen clucked her chicks into the sagebrush while a red-tailed hawk hovered.

There was more to observation than mere pleasure. Down at the Adams Place, another sage-grouse hen led her chicks across the road and up a six-foot road cut. Each of the chicks could stand in a teaspoon, but they attacked the hill with intensity, one after the other, on inch-long legs. The last of the chicks charged the hill, only to tumble backward again and again; finally, it made the summit and darted after its cackling mother.

"I think that one won't make it," came a voice from the back seat, and when I asked why not, the reply was swift and to the point.

"Darwin said so," said Jake.

"Darwin?" I asked.

Yeah," was the gruff response. "Darwin. That guy you always talk about when dumb things die."

"Well, I think it will live," Maggie said, "because we always root for the underdog."

An argument ensued, one of those that must ultimately be decided by a person with some degree of wisdom, or in the absence of such, a parent. In the end, it was decreed that the chick would make it to adulthood, in spite of solid biological arguments to the contrary, because we must always be optimists too.

A few years later, as observation led to science and greater understanding, we came to find those hens and chicks hiked fifteen miles or more to climb the hill we viewed as insurmountable, and they were only halfway on their annual journey to flight, and life. One radio-tagged hen was bred in Government Draw, nested on the east side of the river, and led her brood across the river, two highways, through rural subdivisions, all the while avoiding the normal perils sage grouse encounter on a daily basis.

And again, I found myself wondering what those moments were worth. Clearly, there is no real way to find value in human emotion. A faded photo of a lost friend or worn image of a true love has tremendous value, though it may be worth little on the open market. But what value do we place on clean water, or pollination, oxygen production, or predation? What are river otters really worth?

The hide of a dead river otter is a beautiful thing, sleek, shiny, and soft to the touch. A single hide is worth about $200. A family of five then, is worth $1,000, hanging on the wall. A print of two otters, chosen for the Wyoming Conservation Stamp in 2002, is worth about $400, framed. But, what are river otters worth within a landscape? What is the economic value of their presence, and their role in natural processes? Pelt or painting, should they all end up hanging on walls, we stand to lose more than just otters. We need excited conversations, and grainy photos smeared with fingerprints. We need those Holy Shit! moments.

If otters carry a greater value than the sum of their parts, the habitats they rely upon are no different. We mourn the loss of crucial habitats, but we haven't captured their value any more effectively than we comprehend the worth of a living otter. We lose otters and places for them to live because our economic system has been either unwilling, or incapable of creating effective markets for those "goods and services."

In the case of otters, and natural resources in general, there is a dichotomy between markets for needs and markets for other goods and services, including those we may not completely understand. The price of oil or gas differentiates risk and reward. Markets for cattle and hay, though volatile, allow credible estimation of profit or loss. But, the market for intact aquatic systems is imperfect, at best. Effective management of ranchlands may contribute mightily to water quality, soil stability, sequestration of carbon, and open space, but the market signals ranchers receive are based almost wholly on the price of livestock and hay. Lately, the only other credible economic signal has become the price of land.

All economic systems are driven by cultural demands, whether highly rational, as the need for food or fuel, or highly irrational, like the lust for precious metals. In the days of Tutankhamen, Mao Zedong, or George Bush, markets for goods and services have always been defined by the same forces. Whether those markets are tainted by edict or subterfuge, as in the case of oppressed societies, or poorly understood in freer societies, the demands of the people will ultimately place worth in things we value, and in doing so, create a market to fill that demand.

Allowed to run unchecked or unbalanced, economic systems operate faster than natural systems can recover. China was devastated by Mao's exchange of food and human life for weapons. The American West was altered by people who arrived in a time of incredible rainfall, only to find that reality was extensive drought. European nations only truly valued providers of food when they were starving. Short-term markets can emerge instantly—for pet rocks, or chinchillas—and disappear just as quickly. Other markets seemingly parallel the life of the commodity.

In most cases of market development, partnerships grow out of public demand and private enterprise. Public demand led to development of massive systems for moving people, freight, and mail across the United States. Government incentives and concessions, coupled with private investment, built a rail line across the continent. Without public investment in projects of such immensity, there is no way the railroad would have been built. The same can be said for highways, which evolved from private toll roads, or massive water projects, whether desirable or otherwise.

In North America, market signals on open lands have told businesses primarily to produce food and fiber, with a recent signal placing a high value on residential homesites. At the same time, cultural demands have elevated the values of open space for wildlife habitat, clean water, carbon sequestration, and other goods and services. Until recently, markets had no effective means of capitalizing and valuing conservation, primarily because the potential buyer, the public, had no means of providing capital. The parallels with development of railroads, mail service, water projects, and other large-scale endeavors are inescapable, and the precedent for public and private partnership in market development is well established.

Over time, markets mature. Today, the nation's rail freight system is privately held, efficient, and profitable. Passenger rail ultimately became a service largely funded by government. The mail system evolved from failed private enterprise—to essential government function—to the present system where private enterprise is rapidly forcing the traditional mail system to adapt or become obsolete. That evolution is nearly 200 years old.

As markets develop, they respond to signals. Extremes emerge, especially in early market development. Recent demand for trophy hunting in South Africa has led to release of lions and leopards from captivity, to be hunted as "wild" animals. At another extreme, top-down systems in China led to wholesale harvest of timber, followed by bans on cutting of any timber. Somewhere between capitalistic extremes and radical controls lies the key to development of markets with structure and longevity, an economic radical center.

The final challenge in finding an economic center lies in understanding behavior that defies rational economic models. Simply put, ranchers and farmers behave in a manner diametrically opposed to sound economic judgment. Highly capitalized businesses with narrow returns are generally subject to liquidation. Massive gains in market share invite conversion to cash, and reinvestment. Ranchers have seen costs rise, returns fall, and underlying value soar, and the people who live there still seek ways to maintain the business. People on the land put profits right back into the farm or ranch, whether by reducing debt or expanding operations. Many would be as happy to die in the corral as retire, and that creates problems as well. More than one ranching son or daughter has finally become the boss when they were well past retirement age themselves.

For years, government programs have moved away from regulatory approaches to incentive-based programs that enhance economic opportunity, while at the same time providing habitat enhancement, conservation, and development. In the private sector, habitat-based organizations continue to grow, including foundations dedicated to waterfowl, elk, mule deer, fish, wild sheep, marine life, and other species. Cattlemen and farmers have created land trusts that work in their own backyards. We are all seeking the means to balance cultural desires, economic realities, and ecological opportunities. We are striving to find a radical center. But we have yet to cultivate and maintain real markets for ecosystem services, and until we do so, we will continue to see the erosion of natural systems.

* * *

The Sandhills of Nebraska offer a fascinating study of how some markets work in light of irrational economics. Nearly every operation started out with a 160-acre homestead. Some families survived. Some did not. Some families grew, while others shrank, whether from lack of births, too many deaths, or desires that led youth away from ranching. Though the amount of land

and grass was finite, the need for expansion on one end was filled by contraction on another. A rancher who took care of his land and paid his bills could retire on his investment after a lifetime of hard work, even without radical inflation in land prices. Usually, he could either sell to the next generation, or a neighbor. Almost always, he could live out his life on the place, and watch a new generation flourish.

One Sandhills rancher told me the story of part of his place, a tale of separate original homesteads. In the 1960s, his grandfather was looking to retire. His daughter—the rancher's mother, had married and moved away. She had no real desire or ability to return to the Sandhills, so the grandfather sold a portion of the ranch, and rented the rest, to a neighboring family who needed a place to expand. His grandparents went right on living in the house he grew up in, offering advice to the new owners, picking nits, and enjoying life. The land payments and rent offered them a decent retirement.

The grandson arrived back on the ranch by chance. After his grandparents died, the young man had managed the lease, and when the neighbor was ready to retire, the most logical thing was to buy the place back. Roles reversed, and the young man bought the homestead back, along with the other place. In closing on the ranch, he found that this was the fourth or fifth time the same transaction had taken place. Moreover, he found that in nearly every direction of the compass from his home, the same patterns had prevailed for more than a century. As late as the 1990s, this system continued to work—culturally, economically, and ecologically. The reason it worked is that land values remained rooted in production of perhaps the most traditional and irrational of all commodities—grass.

At the same time, very strange things were happening to ranchers in the West. People in sleepy little places like Cortez, Colorado, or Dillon, Montana, felt like all roads led to their backyard. One friend from southern Colorado said it happened almost overnight. Cars with ski racks, SUVs with bike racks, reggae music, brew pubs, and espresso bars popped out of the ground. Somebody had to drink all that coffee and beer, and in the shadow of mountains, lure of trout streams, and proximity of feng shui red rock, land values skyrocketed. At the same time, many of those who liked their milk steamed and beer stout, weren't overly happy with ranching. In the face of cultural and economic pressures, many ranchers took the money and ran like hell.

Those who sold feng shui needed a place to land, and they had three things left that mattered to them—family, money, and cattle. They didn't need to be close to an airport or fancy restaurant, and they damn sure didn't need a coffee barista in the morning. They needed grass and water, two things abundant in the Sandhills. They also needed a place to put the capital gains earned on their former homes, or their life's work would be taken by the Internal Revenue Service. Suddenly, the market for land in the Sandhills went to levels no one there had ever seen, and the local system came under intense pressure. Fortunately, families old and new maintained a business structure that valued large ranches, and with them, ecosystem-scale natural processes.

In the land of feng shui, the price of land became a beacon that outshone all others, until all others were rendered useless. The "forty acres and mule" once deemed a national ideal, became a reality. This time, it came without the mule, and in many cases, without the mule deer. When the ultimate value of land becomes the view, rock and sky will define the market. But, rock and sky are as inanimate as gold and diamonds. They will never, ever, dance like otters along a stream.

* * *

Otters need three basic things in their lives—food, water, and shelter. Lacking one of the basics, they either explore or die. When they find all three, they are one species that obviously engage in play. Our world is characterized by three driving forces—ecology, economy, and culture. Lacking one of the basics, we too, explore or die. It is not a matter of balance, really, as much as a sense of fairness, that should guide us. Finding a radical center lies in the art, or perhaps the will, to find a level of equity between all three driving forces. Historically, most human systems have tended to hold either economy or ecology somehow "most important," and always at the expense of the other. Many human systems have collapsed. Every one did so because they failed to find that elegant blend of economy and ecology that will ultimately lead to subsequent cultures.

Discovery can be empowering, or frightening. Sometimes, it can be both. Partial discovery is nearly always both, to the extreme. Our understanding of natural process is no better than partial discovery, and the historical record reminds us constantly that we are still learning. Over the course of time, the landscapes of the world have changed in many ways, and they will continue to change. Natural process demands a dynamic world—one that rises and falls to signals we cannot control, or sometimes understand. Tectonic plates, caldera, and climate drive a planet that constantly defies constancy. On a shorter time scale, the processes of disease, fire, herbivory, drought, and flood play an equally powerful role in biological change.

We seem to comprehend there is little we can do to truly affect geological processes. Our understanding of shorter-term processes remains incomplete, and that seems to bother us. In our core, we seemingly accept as fact the notion that meteors may strike, mountains might collapse, or a tsunami can strike us down. At the same time, we seem to blind ourselves to agents like fire and herbivory. We defy natural processes, and sometimes, we tempt fate. For every agent of change, there is a prevailing and countervailing effect. When we curtail fire, we discover the power of fire. When we implement fire, we fear the power of fire. When we do neither, we become pawns of fire.

When we fail to seek, we cease to discover. If we fail to try new things, whether from fear, complacency, or arrogance, we will cease to learn.

It is fascinating to think that we have mapped the great plates that move the face of the earth, found the moxie and the means to travel within the solar system, and still fallen short in our ability to understand our own organism. We've found the ability to manufacture artificial kidney function and forgotten to teach boys to write their name in the snow.

Until very recently, social sciences and history were disregarded, if not disdained, in the natural resource sciences. We spoke of the "art and science" of resource management, then threw away the art and asked the science to answer every question. In many ways, natural resource science was used to exclude humans from the ecosystem. The insight of common people was discarded as blithely as former generations ignored the wisdom of the Shoshone or Crow.

It is a hard road, the one that calls for understanding and respect, but if we truly hope to find a radical center, we must find a way to capture the value of otters in every sense of their being. To do so, we must find relevance between their lives and our own. If the last family of otters held the key to the future of humankind, would we value the places where they lived?

I believe the answer is yes. Moreover, I believe we value those things today, fervently, but we place our faith in legislative and legal forums, when we should be placing our trust in the hands of those who can ultimately make a difference. Quite honestly, otters are worth more to me than hay. If the rancher who grows the hay will continue to grow otters, he or she should be paid for both. He or she should be accorded the highest esteem for his or her care of the public resource, and the system should reward him or her for their effort. We must find the ways and means to maintain traditional economies within natural systems, or we will find ourselves lamenting what we had, instead of celebrating what we have.

We may never "find" the radical center, a concept as elusive and intoxicating as a first kiss. It is more important that we simply keep seeking that elusive, elegant balance. Maybe we need to value patter in the produce aisle more highly than pontification in public. The radical center lies in commitment to the journey more than the outcome, to taking our lumps when they come, and to dancing with joy sometimes, like otters along a stream.

THE CINNAMON MARE

For what it's worth, I'm a cowboy. I have no doctorate in philosophy, but I have known a few good old philosophers in my lifetime. All their lives they maintained that too much of that philosophy just got in the way of common sense, and then all of a sudden, they got old enough to hold court within earshot of young pups like me. Just like that, each of them was transformed into some kind of buckaroo Socrates. And, lucky for me as I see it now, I actually listened to what the old-time cowboys had to say to me. Maybe someday, if I use enough common sense, I'll be able to sit around and act wise, even if I'm not.

Yesterday I rode the cinnamon mare. She's new to the ranch, and to me. That makes us even. The last two days she's been walking the corral fence. Despite the cold, I knew that she and I both needed to be outside. Some days I do better with the cinnamon mare than I do with people. Other days, I leave the cinnamon mare alone. She is a lady, and there are times she's best left to walk the fence. Some days she listens to me, and some days I listen to her. Ours is a cautious relationship.

I seem to listen best to the land when I am horseback. It may be the sense of terrain conveyed by muscle and sinew, as the horse moves through open country. Certainly, much of my sensitivity is tied to the constant signals of the horse's ears, and her greater sense of what is out there, behind the trees, in the rocks, beneath the land. The greater part of sensitivity, though, is more likely the complete vulnerability you feel when life is largely held in the hands of nature, and an animal that outweighs you five or six times over. The old saying goes that if horses knew how puny humans were, they'd stomp us all to death. For whatever reason, most choose to allow us to feel those things we could not otherwise understand.

Today, the red rocks are chuckling. A warm wind blows from the northwest, and molten snow plummets over the rim, cascades of silver, black stains etched into red sandstone where thousands of trickles have come before. In that spot below the rim, there are two springs. One is a short-lived source recharged annually by snowmelt. The other is a deep, geothermal pool that gushes from the earth at thirty gallons each minute. Surely, there is some connection over geologic time and a logical explanation for the occurrence of both. I am content just to know they are there.

Along the creek, snow and ice are breaking up. I'll not have to chop ice for the mare come morning. In the willows a moose lies in the shadows less than 300 yards from the house. She moved in this winter, the first one the old-timers have seen on the creek in a decade. I am hopeful she might stay for the summer too, but I'm not optimistic. More willow and water may keep her close, and as long as the beavers don't back water into the corrals, or take more willows than the creek can stand to lose, they'll keep the water table high. There are new cuttings above and below the house this day, and as much as I like the beavers, the level of activity causes me concern. Sometimes it seems the beavers have a poor sense of balance, and I fear they may eat themselves into oblivion, or leave the creek devoid of shade and places for birds to nest and hide. But, on the whole they are a welcome sight, a sign of health and vitality on the creek, a signal that balance can be achieved on this piece of land.

In the uplands, the mare adopts a leggy trot. I settle into her rhythm and let her move in the direction she chooses. She doesn't like mud or ice, I've found, and I try to follow her line by looking behind me. Some wet day I'll thank her for this track across higher ground. In the junipers on the rim we excite a little bunch of mule deer, and they sneak around the twisted trees like cats peeking out at us as we pass through their domain. This is the first herd of deer I've seen all winter, and it gives me peace to know they have not all disappeared, as gossip in town maintains. We cut a single track on the rim. Lions and the cinnamon mare share disdain for mud it seems. The mare's disdain for lions is entirely one sided.

Far from the stream I look for water—seeps, springs, and little potholes out of the sun's direct stare. This pasture is still filled with grass, mostly bluebunch and needle grass, and it will make good feed for the cattle, which will arrive in early spring. The cows will use it for ten days, maybe twelve at the most, and for that period and the rest of the year, it will be home to others.

The price of this land has exceeded its value for grazing now. Just over the ridge houses light up the night sky. People haul water to these mansions in pickup trucks, and while deer may adapt, the lions do not. The water I seek will not sustain a household, but if we nurture and protect the source, it will help disperse 600 cows and their calves for the brief period they will spend on this piece of ground. We might save snowmelt here and there and tap the spring only so long as the cattle are here. By midsummer it will be parched and dry.

Far below, in the alluvial wake of time, the meadows along the creek are beginning to show traces of green below the receding line of snow. It might be my eyes, for they are anxious to see green. As the mare catches her breath, I study the ditches, easy to pick out by the snow trapped in the shadows of the banks. These ditches, carefully dug following contours of the alluvium, were dug by draft horses and a slip. In an ancient gulch, bleached remnants of a wooden flume glow silver. The land speaks of a single mistake in judgment, an effort to carry water down the slope too fast. The ancient flume speaks of a steward's touch, and now, grass and silt on top of the flume have nearly reclaimed the boards. In the center of the flume runs a single pipe, a more modern solution of conveyance, but one no less a means of saving soil than the one created a century past. The early owners learned quickly of this land, for from that point as far north as I can see, there are no more gullies or flumes. Ditches branch far above the lower meadows, and they move slowly down the slope. There is a lesson I must remember about this soil; mistakes are rarely forgiven.

The importance of water has been ingrained in my mind since I was a boy. Whether chopping ice on a cold morning or chasing a head of water through the mud on sultry summer days, I seem to have inherited four generations of love and understanding for the vitality of hydrogen and oxygen, properly mixed. The power of water is never lost on the cowboy. Slow, soaking rains bring joy and contentment. A good snowpack tempers the difficulty of deep powder and ice on the meadows. Perhaps that is why so many ranchers have a fly rod nestled in a cotton sleeve behind the seat of the pickup.

Cowboys think of water always.

Yesterday water was not so prominent in my mind. The wind was less than charitable, howling down the canyons, driving snow through every crack in the log barn. The wild cats were huddled on my saddle blankets savoring the warmth, and they hissed at me for invading their space and removing their bed. The cinnamon mare stayed in the corner of the shed until she was certain I'd brought oats, and even then she came to me with a great sense of personal sacrifice. The cinnamon mare wears her heart on her sleeve.

Mule deer formed dense, immobile shadows beneath the willows in the creek bottom. A small herd of elk were nearly invisible beneath the red rocks, their vapory breath the only clue that they lay waiting for the sun to track south across the morning sky. Even the chickadees were fluffed into balls, deep inside the hawthorns and sumacs. A single track betrayed a cottontail hidden in the woodpile. Another track belonged to a bobcat holed up at the opposite end of the wood. Yesterday, all of us living here looked to the land for the shelter it had to offer.

My family and I find shelter on this piece of ground, but we are not alone. We know that, and we understand it should be that way. We welcome the communion. The place we live is sheltered, with clean water, but it is not the "best" place in the valley. The best place on this ranch can only be framed by the needs and desires of the user. When a meadowlark sings from a fencepost, he is certain he has found the very best place on the land, or he wouldn't sing. But his singing is no less claim to the land than human claims manifest in laws, and all the laws in the world will not make the meadowlark sing if he is not content. Nor is the meadowlark exclusionary, for in the wake of his crystalline aria countless other birds manifest their own sense of joy. There is the slap of a beaver tail on the water, the howl of a coyote, the motherly bawling of a cow, and irreverent squeals of my own children. If we can learn to share the land and to care for the needs of others, materially and spiritually, we can begin to see the land as a part of ourselves and not a prize to be won.

Ownership is important. Whether by fee title or spiritual bond, ownership is critical to stewardship. But with ownership must come respect and responsibility. If spiritual ownership ends at the moment rapture passes, then spiritual ownership is not enough. The test of ownership lies in loving that land as much when it is covered in ice and snow, or blown desolate with drought, as when rolling hills are capped by waves of wildflowers. Most of this ranch is owned by the people of the nation, but that must not change or alter the way I view the land. To succumb to such would render me incapable of caring for the place as a whole. Most of us rarely admit such, but the land may own us far more than we own the land.

In finding shelter on this piece of land, my family and I accept the responsibility of sharing it with other creatures. Whether trained in ecology or immersed in it by reality, as is the rancher, most of us on the land understand the minutiae to which we are reduced by countless other forms of life upon which we depend. My children are the sixth generation on the land, but yesterday as we watched a bobcat dance in the snow, I wondered how many generations of those cats have shared the land with one of our own. How many more generations of bobcats and cowboys might share this piece of ground?

At rest in the saddle, I can feel the land undulate beneath the mare, but I sense more than rock, sinew, and chinook. At the heart of wondering lies the soul of our own value system. What gifts can we truly offer to those whose wide eyes sparkle beneath broad brimmed hats, or those whose eyes watch us from the shelter of the red rocks? I believe we strive to offer a better place than which we found, a place where life and vitality are no less, and maybe even greater. Perhaps therein lies the reason I toil and fret over the landscape on which I live. The true measure of the gift lies not in the value of the land. The important thing lies in how we choose to value land.

To a cowboy the single most important value in the land is its ability to sustain native grasses, forbs, and shrubs. Year after year. Cash values may exponentially surpass the true reward of bluebunch seedlings, but so long as springtime brings a flush of green to yellow-gray sagebrush hillsides, cash values dim and fade. My greatest measure of success lies not in how I use the grass, but in how I am able to leave it each year and in the amalgamation of years I am able to care for the land. Grass may be much less valuable to the rancher for its economic value than for the spiritual rendering it leaves in the soul. Purely economic, as bankers must sometimes be, grass properly managed means sustainable business over the long haul. Purely ecological, as most ranchers prefer to be, grass tells us how the land senses our touch long before other signs of joy or despair become apparent. Grass provides the basic habitat for many, many lives not human. But, in sensual reality, it is plants, and especially grass, that rejuvenates the soul.

The cinnamon mare is anxious for her head, and I give it, for my own head is drifting beyond the scope of my sight. As the mare picks her way from red rock to snow-covered slopes of phosphoria and limestone, I sense some of the gifts left to me by old cowboys. I am saddened I was never able to tell them I finally understand some of the knowledge they tried to share. The filly is anxious, as I have been, as my own children often seem. For once I feel my own patience rising. In its grandeur and immensity, the short ride from one side of the canyon to the other is more than I can ever comprehend, and yet, if I am to succeed in living with this piece of ground, I must do more than simply comprehend. I must begin to understand, and in doing so, must take the time to tell of what I learn. More than that, I must recognize that the landscape will change over time, and nothing I might try can overcome the power of the land itself. My opportunity lies in adapting to change and evolving with realities presented by things I cannot understand.

Most of what I know of the land and of the values that reside within myself I have learned on the land. On good days the land lives within me, and I am able to give myself back. Now I think that is what my parents sought so desperately to share with me. And when I was patient enough to sit and listen to those older than me, I was offered grains of knowledge earned in a lifetime of rides on cinnamon mares. The land was not always kind. Tears of those broken by a piece of ground stain my fingers yet, and I still taste the salt of their pain on my lips. When I worry about the land and my care for it, it seems I can see every set of eyes blown dry by wind both hot and cold. I am frightened by what the land can do to mortality; even those most indomitable have been withered when they chose to fight. And yet, I see most often the nurturing, patient eyes of those who have made the land the ultimate guide of their enterprise in life. These are the men and women from whom I hope to learn. These are the people whose spirit rises in me on the truly good days.

The filly is into her element now. Her trot rises and falls as if she is adrift on a favorable current. I find my thoughts there. A hundred rides rush back to me. Three hundred miles away. Bob Wright is pointing out a bobolink, a titmouse, a waving stand of sedge amidst whitecaps of sage. Stan Flitner's eyes burn azure in the shimmering heat of Red Gulch, and I see him pointing out every single new plant, nearly falling off his horse to see that it is true, that his care for the land has created such a response. Mildred Miller stands regally next to me. She is confident and serene as she explains the harsh realities of making a living with the land. I feel the bitter cold in the midnight hour, engine off and only moonlight as Gary and Nancy Espenscheid pour out their excitement about caring for the land holistically. My father's hand is on my shoulder, and he whispers to me to watch; more than 200 bighorn ewes and lambs graze within reach of the shelter we have found in the rocks. My father's father is alive again, and he is leading me into the willows to find a fifteen-petal rose, a single strange variant he noticed in nearly four square miles of rose bushes and willows. Bill Hancock is sitting on the board seats in the sale barn, and the history of the land and its people pour out above the excited clatter of the auctioneer. Ron Vore stands waist deep in a beaver pond, casting deftly, chuckling. Pearl Spencer wanders another red canyon with me. Ninety years from birth, nearly a century of this piece of the world, she stills reveres living things with the anxiousness of a child. Now nearly blind, she seems to discern wildflowers by scent, a voice on the breeze. My sense of the land is mine, and mine alone, but there are so many others living with my definition of the land that it transcends human reality. My challenge is to help carry on the tradition of stewardship ingrained in generations of ranchers, and to share those values with others who will listen. This is not easy work. I have barely begun to understand the cinnamon mare.

Often I am asked if other ranchers feel this way about the land. Some do not. That is evident. But the ranchers I have known for a lifetime have taught me these values. Some of my learning has been active, as sharp as the sting of a lariat across the shoulders. Very few of the ranchers I know enunciate their feelings, for they have learned to hold these matters closely. When you allow others to view the underside of your values, you open them to ridicule or challenge by others. It is easier to gallop into a biting wind than to be chastised or denigrated for beliefs that shape your life. I talk of the land and its influence on the soul with many cowboys, and always, there is a soft calm that must precede and characterize the discussion. Speaking of the land is not taken lightly when soil, water, and vegetation frame life's failures and dreams.

A nasty wind drives us from the ridge behind the house, and the mare drifts easily back toward the ranch. She isn't anxious, nor is she reluctant. It's been a good day, but we are both ready to be home. At the barn, her back is dark, streaked with sweat beneath the saddle. Steam curls into the blue light of the evening. The mare nickers when I head to the barn, and I rub her down slowly, a luxury for both of us. She closes her eyes and rubs her hard forehead against my shoulder, then nips at my elbow. She's earned her oats this day, but I linger. Instead of filling the bucket and letting her clean it herself, I feed her handfuls at a time. The mare lingers too, it seems, playing me for attention. In the quiet, reflected light of winter evening, I am content with this land, with this place I call home.

The aroma of dinner drifts down the hill, and in the frigid stillness, every word from mother to son is amplified. A three-foot-tall man steps off the porch, casts a nine-foot shadow across the snow, and then he is buried in a drift as deep as his chest. The cinnamon mare looks his way and nickers. Her ears are up now, and the boy slogs through the snow, carrot ensconced within a red mitten. The mare nickers again. I will never understand the magic that exists between horses and small children, but maybe I am not meant to understand such things. My friend Tony Malmberg says it is quite simple. When a little kid catches a horse or gives him oats, it's because the kid likes the horse. When bigger cowboys do it, they want something from the horse.

The boy leads the mare into the corral; she resting her very nose on the snow so that he can remove the halter. His shadow has been absorbed by sunset, but he remains nine feet tall. We start our journey to the house, and as much as I long to reach down and hold him, I resist. Halfway, his legs grow weary, and he asks me to carry him. My own legs are light and strong. I will never forget this evening—this place, this feeling. In the darkness behind me, the mare nickers again. The boy is sound asleep in my arms.

As I watch her dark shape move down to the creek, I wonder if this place is special somehow to the cinnamon mare. Does she sense her contribution to the boy who sneaks her carrots from the kitchen? In the depth of winter, we lean on one another, and we learn the land together. Her ancestors were here long before my own, but this piece of ground has brought us together. I wonder if there is a place on the ranch where the cinnamon mare finds her own sense of place. I suspect there are many.

My own sense of place is not centric and cannot be so. For me to focus on a single place would be to ignore all other pieces of the landscape. In the winter I am drawn to south-facing slopes where sunlight is gathered. In the heat of summer deep glades of aspen provide escape from the same blistering sun. Every day there is a new place on a ranch to be discovered and felt. Most of them are not new at all. I may have failed to pay proper attention, or maybe that one day, the land chose to show me its heart. In living on this land, and caring for the soil, plants, and creatures both wild and domestic, my sense of mortality is heightened by the reality that I will never know the land as well as some might wish or claim. The reason ranchers continue to grow grass and cattle in the face of acceleration of land prices is because they cannot imagine a life where every day is the same. A cowboy likes the land. It matters not whether conditions produce mesquite and sideoats grama or tall grasses that brush the bottom of the stirrups. While no two days or pieces of ground can ever be the same, there is constancy in being on the land, an incredible connection with life's diversity that drives us through the day. Every morning holds new fortune, some good, some not so good, but no two are ever the same.

A fire crackles in the living room. Outside, not a single light blinks, save countless stars. The moon is a recluse. On the wall of my office hangs a map of the ranch and the land beyond those borders. My eye is drawn to the other side of the Continental Divide, to a place where my family has ranched for six full generations. Buried bones are all that remain of the early ones, though their names are affixed to creeks and streets. That is not enough it seems, to mark a family's passing. In every generation hence has come grim optimism, a desire to hold and nurture the land around us, to let it fall asleep in our arms. It would be easy to declare those homesteads and ranches somehow sacred, to say that they would be treated with the same degree of love and attention my great-great-grandfather felt. But to do so would be to err as much in retrospect as arrogant declarations of immortal superiority would be today. How can we possibly choose a most important place if we truly see the land as the vast amalgamation of life that it truly represents?

My interaction with this land is successional. If I can be a source of energy to coax living diversity in a positive direction, to retain nature's treasures, then my time will be well spent. My attachment to the land is not permanent, nor is it temporary.

It is both. In sharing this land with cinnamon mares, cows and their calves, golden-eyed bobcats, and darting bluebirds, I must seek balance every day. In handing this piece of land to my children, I offer only opportunity, not immortality. From the moment the sun blooms over the Nugget Sandstone until it blushes and hides behind Limestone Mountain, I try to think and act for tomorrow, and appreciate the day at hand.

I make mistakes. Some I make more than once. But the land is patient with me, and sometimes I actually believe the land feels my intent, just as the cinnamon mare senses the heart of my child. Somewhere between geologic time, human mortality, and the longevity of a wonderful mare lies reality.

* * *

Six months ago, the cinnamon mare and I shared a day in the stillness of winter, as if time stood still. Like the night sky, my thoughts were crystalline, sharp, and patient. The next morning would bring new learning, new opportunity, and new life. But the next morning brought no rain, and there was none after that. Now, folks say it is the driest year ever. Thick red dust coats every millimeter of our lives. Hot wind drives it beneath the doors and around the windows. Grasses that should still be hiding within themselves are headed out, withered and spent. The cows are anxious, and the meadows are tanned. The first day of summer is still a month away.

This morning, I'm riding the roan filly, Muffin. She is bigger than the cinnamon mare, and she glides across the land with a feminine grace that belies her youth. She is all business, this one. She doesn't know this piece of ground yet, but she learns quickly, and she never forgets. Maybe she is lucky to have missed the winter, for she has no frame of reference from which to complain. Today, she is my favorite horse in the pen.

More than 100 species of birds are here for the summer, among them tiny wrens that flit about, then turn their tail feathers to the blue sky when they perch on the log pile outside the kitchen. They remind me of my wife. Today, they are the birds most special. Yesterday, a drumming ruffed grouse held my favor.

On Greenough Mountain, a trio of pronghorn fawns burst out of the sagebrush and spook Muffin, then scatter in three plumes of dust. Their mother stamps her feet at me and wheezes through her nose. They are my favorites too.

And at the end of the day, even a plant caught my attention, one I never saw on the land. In a tiny vase above the sink rose a single sego lily, a fragile white whisper from my three-year-old son to his mother. It is a gift of the land through the fingers of a child. It is magnificent. Neither flower nor boy will remain the same, but my memory of this day will not wane. In the heart of drought, the land has rekindled my soul.

FROGGY WENT A COURTIN'
AND HE DID RIDE

J ake was about ten, too young to get a job and too old to sit around the house. This is a deadly combination with young boys, likely the main reason things like baseball and basketball were invented. We were standing next to a spring-fed pond the size of a living room, and the Montana sun was slinking behind the curvature of the earth with a slow retreat you only get to see on vast expanses of prairie. There was a half ball of brilliant light, and an arc of landscape; if you glanced to the west, it was enough to confuse the brain into believing the world was really black and white.

We were there to help out my friend Linda Poole, who had taken on the challenge of managing a spectacular landscape, an amalgamation of eons of geology and ecology that collided into the plains of northern Montana. Linda asked me to come up and look around, meet the neighbors, and compare notes on management. I was anxious for a look at that country, and Jake was always an affable companion. The day before, we wandered north along ancient Indian trails and old cattle driveways, crossing the Yellowstone and the Missouri, backtracking Lewis and Clark, and zooming down the gigantic waterslide outside Billings.

This day, we'd hiked and driven across the shortgrass. We stood on every ridge and hunched in most of the swales. We stared at maps, identified grasses and forbs, and ate greasy burgers in the tiny town of Zortman for lunch. It was a perfect spring day, with hot sun one minute, and teeth-chattering snow the next. And now, we were on the banks of an ancient pond.

Linda and I were deep in thought when we noticed Jake had immersed himself waist deep in the black water, totally oblivious to all the jabber of the day. His sleeves were wet to the armpits, and his chin was millimeters above the brine.

Linda asked what he was doing, a bit worried.

"He's catching frogs and turtles," I said. "I think it's hardwired."

"You have a genetic command that directs you to catch frogs and turtles?" she asked.

"Yep," I nodded, "that, and light shit on fire."

Jake retreated from the pond with a grin on his face, belly exposed, shirt doubled up in his hands. It was getting really cold, but that was never an issue with this kid, especially while we stood and examined each of a dozen frogs and four turtles, allowing Jake to release each into the pond after we checked them out. Linda congratulated him on his ability, and said he was as efficient as a sandhill crane. Jake's dirty face lit up, and Linda was charmed.

Linda headed to the warm truck, and I told her to wait. Jake hung his head and took a frog from one pocket and a turtle from the other and let them go.

"Hardwired," I shrugged.

"You can come back any time," she smiled, and Jake got the biggest steak at dinner.

* * *

When I was his age, I had what must have been the biggest frog ranch in the western United States. At its peak, my spread was four big washtubs connected by rock and wood bridges and filled to the max with an assortment of frogs and toads that I have never been able to find since then. There were the little singers, and big leopard frogs, but there were gray toads with multicolored bumps, and black toads that might have been frogs. In the water, I had batches of pollywogs and other frog-like creatures.

Grandma was the real genius of the frog ranch. She was the one who figured out to put a little piece of stinky garbage on a rock right at the water's surface to attract flies, thus inventing the first amphibian self-feeder. She could see the frog ranch from the kitchen window, and kept cats and birds off the toad range, just as she blasted bobcats and coyotes out of the chicken house.

At the end of the summer, I was expected to get the frogs to the creek and let them go, and I always did, but a few seemed to end up in my room, in a stolen dish, croaking at night and scaring the living hell out of my sisters.

When I got older, my first paying job was irrigating, and for a frog hunter, irrigation was the equivalent of Africa. There

were frogs in the ditches, frogs in the creek, frogs in the meadows, and frogs on the road. I never really outgrew the desire
to catch frogs, but there were so damn many it seemed like I
could never keep up. Above me, long-billed curlews squawked
and dove, and all around me, sandhill cranes jumped and
called. In the tall grass, I would chase out weasels, coyotes, and
bobcats. I assumed they all ate frogs, and yet, the cacophony
of croaking continued. The song of frogs put me to sleep at
night, and when I woke in the mornings, the sound of frogs
was still there.

* * *

Late June, many years later, I was baking in the heat of a Bighorn
Basin afternoon, back-riding a pasture the size of Rhode Island,
looking for a handful of cows and calves that had escaped previous scrutiny by dozens of riders. "Back-riding" is the chore of
finding strays, escapees, and other critters that avoid detection.
I have back-ridden in an airplane, and watched cattle dart into
dense stands of brush to avoid being seen. In the same plane, we
circled and radioed to horsemen, who rode within roping distance of cattle that hid beneath the canopy. The riders insisted
there were no cattle.

I was riding with Stan Flitner, a man I admired then and
now, and we were looking for ten cows and their calves. He
rode high and I rode low, one on the ridgeline, the other in the
draws, checking every spring and seep, every water tank, and
every hidey-hole. By the end of the day, we had found four pair,

and Stan declared the rest either lost, dead, or already captured and not counted.

Red Gulch was a desert in the truest sense; it was the toilet for Alkali Basin, a desert in itself. At the bottom of the landscape, Red Gulch was a mineral maelstrom of eroded alkaline mud, oxidized bluffs of ancient iron, windblown sand, and erosion pavement left over from violent summer thunderstorms that tore soil away and left only the rocks too large to roll or float. Riding up from the bottom of the draw, the size of the rocks on the ground increased in size, from pebbles to marbles, to golf balls. On one side of the draw, the rocks were igneous orbs; on the other, they were decaying bits of sandstone. Ancient sea meets volcano.

At the time, it felt like volcano. Even early in the season, the temperatures were in the high nineties, and after a full day of traversing Rhode Island to find eight bovines, I'd had enough. And, I was lost. Thankfully, the sun was setting in the west, which was the direction of the truck, and I let my horse have her head and stared into the sun.

Within a mile or so, I saw Stan headed up the ridge from the north, and decided I was either not lost, or we both were. I reined in and waited for him, beached on an ancient reef.

"You know what I miss?" Stan said, when we joined up.

I could have given twenty answers and been right on each of them.

"Frogs," he said.

That was not one of the answers on my list.

"I miss frogs," he went on, as Stan is wont to do, with a soliloquy about frogs that took us three miles to the truck. My part in the conversation was mostly to grunt, but I found myself checking pockets for frogs, thinking about what Stan was saying, and dreaming about a frog ranch I once had.

"They were everywhere," he said when we got back to the ranch. "I could stand here and hear frogs all the time. I heard them when I went to sleep, and I heard them when I woke up."

We walked up from the barn, with alkali and red dirt in our hair and our eyes and our pores. Our skin was drier than paper, and Stan was still talking about frogs.

"I think we need more frogs," he decided, and his spurs jingled up the bone-dry road to the house.

* * *

When my family moved to Red Canyon Ranch, the silence at night was deafening. Oh, there were coyotes and owls, winds coming up and down the ridges, cattle and horses. There was the steady chuckling of the creeks working their way down grade, but in spite of water coursing through every valley, and hundreds of acres of meadows under water, we never heard a frog.

The most disturbing aspect of the lack of sound was how much it bothered me. I could deal with a lot of things at the time, and I needed to deal with a lot of things at that moment. There were a wife and three little kids, hired help, public notions of what was right and wrong, federal agencies, budgets, bulls, calving percentages. I spent my days digging postholes some-times, and going to meetings other times, but when the sun ended the day and the nighthawks and bats began their shifts, I thought about frogs.

Worldwide, the number of amphibians was seemingly in decline, and there were a gazillion reasons, it seemed. There were those who insisted that blue-eyed humans were the sole cause, and there were others who offered complex theories about global warming, chemical contamination, predation, and a plethora of other notions. Science didn't add to the solution. Instead, it seemed scientists only fueled a blazing debate, the root of which was who was most culpable.

The only reality I had was a lack of frogs singing in the night.

If there were a gazillion reasons for a worldwide decline, there were about as many in this valley outlined by cliffs of sandstone. Some of those I could address, and some were beyond my control or comprehension. Drought was unchangeable. Maintaining water where water should be plentiful was not.

The landscape around me was built to shed water and soil. Bottomlands caught every element, and captured them, but only if the pieces were in place. This landscape was an ancient relic of vast seas and beaches formed into sandstone ridges, some once immersed, others blasted by wind and sun since the earliest geologic times. The grand design for this place on earth was for mountains to fall and valleys to rise.

Throughout the basin, relics of multiple glacial ages poked out of the valley floor. Some were apparent. Some were elusive. From the bottom of the canyon, it was impossible to see the layers of rock, but on top of the remaining rocks, ages and times popped up like prairie dogs. Geologists found no less than six different periods of erosion, some nothing more than a sandstone knob in the middle of dolomite or phosphoria.

"This landscape has been through hell and back," Dave Love grinned. "Hell, it's been turned upside down and over again. After that, it went through the Ice Age, which was really a bunch of cold periods. This is a glorious mess."

The key to the geological and ecological balance of Red Canyon was the ability of long narrow streams to carry massive flows of water, or little water at all. Fire and ice, freeze and thaw. None of this was new to frogs.

Frogs evolved by adapting to wet periods where they could lay eggs in the damp soil and leave them waiting for rain. Eggs were laid in backwater eddies, flooded plains, buffalo wallows, ditches, and basements. Like the seeds of upland grasses, eggs of amphibians were opportunistic, and above all, patient. When it got wet again, out popped frogs, salamanders, and toads.

In the interim, amphibians didn't disappear entirely. Major rivers, big wetlands, and perennial streams had the habitat necessary for frogs to emerge annually. The crescendos may be less intense, but the songs should still be there.

Aside from the drought, and maybe the effects of fertilizer, the greatest challenge to the frogs I wasn't hearing was the fact that what little water we had was hotfooting it down valley in a hurry. Most mountain and canyon streams have only two ways to absorb the intense energy of water running at blast force. One is to spread across the valley floor in a snakelike path that steals energy. The other is for beavers or debris to capture the energy in deep pools and step the power down one dam at a time. Given time and the right kind of soils, there becomes no broad valley to wander across. The only harness for a runaway stream becomes a healthy population of beavers. But beavers can't do all the work alone. Hillsides and meadows have to catch water and hold it long enough to let it percolate straight down, and not run downhill. Little streams have to sort rock and gravel, and plants have to drink deeply from every rain or thaw. If I wanted to hear frogs sing, I had to keep water from leaving the canyon.

* * *

For three long years, everything we did centered on growing willows along streams, carpeting steep hillsides with native grasses, and holding water on the meadows. Irrigation systems were improved to deliver more water and hold it longer. Hay yields went up. Red dirt was almost absent from the stream when it reached the river. Little puddles lived into the late summer and reemerged with the first fall rain. Calves were heavier. Cows bred more readily. Moose wintered in the bottomlands, and beavers were plentiful enough to trap some and send them to other ranches. But, not a single frog would sing.

On the 12th day of August, in the year of 1998, *anno Domini*, when Jake was seven and Maggie was five, a leopard frog hopped into Red Canyon Creek. Not one of us saw the frog hit the water, but I knew exactly what it was.

"Frog!" I yelled, and I ran for the creek.

Jake and Maggie charged through the willows like coyotes, their faces painted with mud and blood, and we arrived at the water's edge together. I eyed the creek, and the kids eyed me, sure that I had gone as mad as a prairie widow. Suddenly, Jake leaped from the streambank like he was thrown, and splashed in the water like a cub bear. When he turned around, he had a leopard frog in his hands, and a smile on his face.

Maggie hopped in with him, and they danced around like they had never seen a frog in their lives. Maggie held the frog, and gave it back to Jake, and he gave it to me, and I handed it back so he could return it to the creek. We sloshed into the house for lunch and announced our find to a receptive audience that took the afternoon off from digging postholes and spent it hunting frogs, but mostly, drinking beer.

If we had one frog, there had to be more, and there were. We found frogs at Deep Creek, and all over Cherry Creek. There were frogs along the river, and frogs in the meadows. Joe found a salamander in a pond at Cinnamon's Meadow, and the dogs found a toad in the yard. We heard frogs at night, and more than once, I had to remove them from "lost" serving dishes that found their way under beds in children's rooms. We had frogs, and if we had frogs, we had a system that was working.

* * *

When we gathered in the fall, I found myself riding next to a neighboring rancher, a great guy, and a hell of hand. I was a little lost for what to talk about, even though I had left a half gallon of whiskey in his pickup to thank him for all his help. He didn't mention the whiskey, and he seemed a little dismayed to be seen with me, but we gathered a ton of his cows and headed them down the road toward home. I was intimidated, and unsure of what to say.

"We have frogs," I said, completely out of the blue.

There was a long silence in which I expected Walt to gallop off, far away from me, but he trotted along on his big gray horse, keeping pace with my bay.

"You're lucky," he smiled. "When I was a kid, we had frogs everywhere . . ."

THE SMELL OF DIRT

The scent of South Piney dust hit me when I stepped out of the truck. One slight misstep—a boot toe under a clump of grass—and breeze enough to send the dust upward. The perfume of soil was intoxicating; my mind wandered through decades. I hadn't smelled that dirt for thirty years, and even then, only a time or two, when I rode over the hill from the north to pick up some cattle that paid no heed to signs on fences and lines on maps.

The odor was frightening, and exciting at the same time. I steadied myself with a hand on a parked truck and shook my head like a cat with a hairball, fighting cobwebs and reality at the same time. It has been said that smell is the most intense and longest lasting of our senses. At that moment, my other senses were absent, leaving smell as the victor.

Just over the hill, on another ranch, in another time, I found out much about what would be important to me in life, and who I might become. At the time, I was the size of a bale of hay. I actually weighed less than some bales—about ninety pounds. And, at five foot three, I could actually hide behind a bale stood on end. I was seventeen years old, going into my senior year in high school, with one year of experience on the

ranch behind me. That was a year marked with blood and scars
and failures, a split vote on whether I should be rehired or not.
As one of my bosses said to me and anyone else who would listen, I "wasn't much."

Sooner or later, you have to learn about honesty. In my
case, I learned it first as a recipient of truth.

Joe and Ruth Budd were elder statesmen then, something a lot of people never understood. Joe was a former
legislator, a leader in the cattle industry, one of the premier
breeders of Hereford cattle in the world, and still full of piss
and vinegar. I was back on the ranch because he wanted me
back on the ranch, and the deal with the devil held that if he
wanted me, by God, he had to have me eating at his table.

Ruth set that table, and you never, ever, entered it with a
hat on your head. I sat once, and she knocked my hat off with
a spoon, missing the hat cleanly and leaving a duck egg on my
gourd. Some things you learn through subtlety, but that lesson
was immediate.

The kitchen was always filled with smoke, and Ruth never
burned the food. The only outside voice was Paul Harvey's, at
noon. When Paul was done, the radio was turned off, and political
banter began. Political banter ended at about one, when Joe had a
nap, and I was sent back out to work. Work was an olio act—irrigation, fencing, moving cattle, packing salt, unpacking groceries,
shoeing horses, carpentry, logging—no day was the same.

Whatever I lacked in stature and strength, I began to
find I could make up for in other ways. I found an incredible

understanding that my life was a part of this landscape, maybe only a cog in a wheel, but what I did went far beyond the daily chores, or the challenges faced in completing a task. There was a whole world here. I was part of a community, one made up of two older people and me, but one in which deer, moose, fish, birds, and cattle also lived.

There is much more to a community than the things that arrange themselves on any given day. Over the course of months, I found myself immersed in family, history, ecology, and human relations. At lunch, Joe's commentary on the news was a highlight of the day, and I found that in challenging his views, I was better informed, if not more appreciated. We fought and argued, and in doing so, he began to share the history and culture of three generations. When he was full of shit, I said so. He said I was full of shit all the time, but when I was occasionally proven right, he would admit as much. Those were usually days I got to clean the outhouse.

After one long day moving cattle, we unsaddled by the ancient, low-built log barn, and I dreamed about just letting the horses out so that I might get to supper. Joe looked at me, read my mind, and growled.

"Horses don't eat, you don't eat," he said, and so I stayed, scooped out their oats, and watched as they ate them slowly. I was tired, but my mind was alive, and wide open.

In the twilight, other members of the community emerged. Sandhill cranes rasped and leopard frogs croaked songs from the bog. Trout surfaced in the creek, slapping their tails as they captured bugs on the surface. Deer began to wander from the dry hills to the meadows, and an owl floated silently over the yard. Nighthawks and bats dove on bugs, and a cow moose led her calf past the barn.

One by one, I took the horses to the pasture, learning a little more about each as we walked.

Ruth scolded me for being late to dinner, but she fed me anyway.

Joe gave me a cold beer.

So goes life.

Just over the hill from this place where the smell of dirt left me nostalgic and nearly incapacitated, what I was learning was an ethic of conservation. We railed at environmentalists, stood in bewilderment at the Rainbow Family gathering up the road, fought the neighbors, and cursed the government. And yet, in our fear and suspicion of things that were new or different, we were consistent in our love of the place where we were, and in our belief that it was a special place.

In that community, things often disconnected collided in a massive world of reality. Unabashed wonder in things we cannot comprehend is only found when we quit parsing and dissecting the unknown and learn to simply enjoy the reality. A red bird is red. Do we really need to know why?

Perhaps the most important thing I found in the dirt on the other side of the hill is humility. Wonder and humility come from the same place, from things we don't completely comprehend. When we ignore the wonder, or exert our will, we find that the world is much bigger than ourselves. We realize that other things depend on us, much as we depend on other things. We fear not the owl in the night sky, or the hawk in daylight. We become aware of both and pity the mice.

What I found was a sense of place, a sense of self, and a sense of community, and those qualities are the essence of that thing we call "conservation." Badger Clark wrote it best in his classic "A Cowboy's Prayer."

> *Make me as big and open as the plains,*
> *As honest as the hawse between my knees,*
> *Clean as the wind that blows behind the rains,*
> *Free as the hawk that circles down the breeze!*

Conservation is many things, not a single thing. It is not the role of one person to explain or interpret the meaning of conservation to others. Each will have their own moments of wonder and humility. It may be a sunset, a hard wind, freezing rain, fire, or greening grass. All are interconnected, and all are a part of who we are, or wish to be.

Conservation is visceral, something in our gut. It is the smell of South Piney dirt, the taste of Middle Piney water, and the deep understanding that the two are vastly different, though one hill apart. We don't choose to see the difference or not—it is something we find in our bones, our memory, and our soul. When you work in the dirt, the soil finds its way into your being. It comes through pores opened to dismiss sweat, through membranes in the nose and eyes. Even the most hardened of callused hands crack enough to let the land seep into the bloodstream. Once in the blood, the hardest hearts are defenseless against the dirt.

Some people stay. Some people leave. Willa Cather wrote incredible stories of both reverence and despair. Some prairie men and women found wonder and hope in the grasslands. Others went insane. We will never know the dirt that found the hearts of those people. Was it the soil left behind, or the dust beneath their feet?

Conservation is intensely personal. We will never conserve landscapes without respect for those who have lived on the same place before our time. Working on the land is a vocation of the heart, and sometimes, solely of the heart. Every person who stays on a piece of ground finds love for that place. We become an essence in the perfume of dirt beneath our feet. We are absorbed by the land, and at the same time, we absorb the essence of soil, vegetation, water, and air.

Conservation isn't free. For every well-managed habitat, choices must be made, and sometimes, those choices are agonizing. There was a time not long ago when economic realities largely dictated a single truth on the landscape. Scale of operations, family dynamics, costs and returns, and community values were logical considerations. Those things determined who would own the land for the time being, not what would happen on the land. Grouse and mule deer, bobcats, weasels and wrens, and even cattle and sheep could breathe pretty easy in that world.

In the last few decades, the choice to operate a ranch or farm, and to maintain, by default or choice, open space and wildlife habitat, has become economically flawed, even illogical. Land split into small pieces is worth a fortune. A friend in central Wyoming bought 160 acres for $20,000 in the early 1960s and had to fight like heck to find a banker who would take the risk to loan him three-fourths of that amount. Now, he fights off bids to subdivide the place for a hundred times the purchase price. His children are far away, and none plan to return.

"What the hell do I do?" he asked me one day. "I had a ranch back then, and I still make money on my hay, but I don't need money. Our kids don't need money, but none of them are coming back here."

His voice trailed off, and I wondered what it was that bothered him so much. He pointed out the window to the north, where a sagebrush hillside undulated down to his meadows. In the late light of day, deer poured from the dry hillside over his fences like quicksilver.

"This meadow is all those deer have left," he sighed. "I just don't want to go out of this life thinking the deer will have nowhere left to winter."

In all directions from his ranch, houses dotted the landscape. You could tell the new from the old, not by design or weathering, but by location of the houses. The first settled near the creek to be out of the wind and close to water; those most recent built massive homes on the very tops of the hills, to see and be seen. Even at night, the valley was awash in light and sound. As we stood on the porch, an argument broke out somewhere up the creek, and we could hear every word.

"We sure as shit never had that in 1969," he said, and the door clapped behind him. An old border collie walked me to my truck, and watched cars race by on the road.

"He used to chase every damned car," I heard from the front room. "But, that was only a couple a day."

The old dog licked my hand and wandered back into the yard.

* * *

Today was Father's Day, and when I asked my sixteen-year-old daughter if she wanted to go out to Red Canyon, she smiled and asked if she could drive. I was stunned.

It was my first trip back to a place I loved, a landscape I knew as intimately as the creeks and aspen stands along Piney Creek. In a year with rains like I had never seen, and likely never will again, the landscape was expressive, and spectacular. Green grass and red rocks were interspersed with a rainbow of wildflowers, with colors that have no names.

When we stopped at Foster Draw, Maggie took a deep breath and kicked the dirt.

"I could never have a white outfit when we lived here," she said to her mother, "and now I see why."

In her hand was a wad of red dirt, and her hand went straight to her nose.

"I love the smell of this place," she said. "This is where I grew up."

Hope springs eternal.

FROM THE LAND

Thousands of years ago, Shell Creek ran out of granite rocks and began carving its way through soft soils between the canyon and the Big Horn River. Rocks and roots tried to hold the soil, but the water was stronger. Beavers tried to slow the stream, but the water was stronger. In the long run, the meandering stream found a course through the fine dirt, until now, when it runs directly to a riverbed lined with rock that the water will eventually defeat.

As the stream found a path of least resistance, cottonwood seedlings sprouted on sandbars dumped by torrents of spring. Shrubs and grasses found respite as the water level reached a constant point below, and meadows developed. Where the stream once meandered, oxbow ponds remain, gathering water from rain, snow, and occasional floods. Thickets opened into wetlands lined by cattails and bulrushes, plants tall enough that deer have worn ancient paths beneath the canopy. On cold days, steam rises from open water until fog hangs low over the swamps. Deer like it here. There is water, feed, and cover. There are paths of escape the deer know by heart, and there are places so thick that escape is unnecessary.

Pheasants, ducks, geese, and yellow-headed blackbirds all find this place to their liking. Rabbits like it here, as do the coyotes, foxes, and bobcats that follow them into the swamp. On the branches of the trees and shrubs, tiny birds move constantly: chickadees, sparrows, flycatchers, and others so swift they are but blurs of color and noise. Raccoons and mink abound near the water's edge. There are bugs and plants without easy names, some in the water itself, others in the black, gummy mud that makes up the bottom of this place.

This piece of ground is part of a ranch. On the place above, the land is the same, as are the ranches on down the creek. None of this land is for sale. None of this land is farmed. Farmland is valued as high as $600 an acre in the basin, and this could be prime farm ground. Instead, it is called "waste and bog" on the tax rolls. The ranchers on Shell Creek use this land in the wintertime, a place where cows and their babies can get out of the cold wind. It is grazed, which is part of the reason the swamp remains open, and as a result, it is home to hundreds of species of wild things.

For all of this, the ranchers receive no money. Sometimes, on hard days, they look at the swamp and think about how much the land might bring if it were farmed, but for generations, none have ever done more than look. For one thing, the swamp wouldn't be there for cows in the winter. Maybe more importantly, there is a certain sense of satisfaction just knowing that the critters are out there.

On Middle Piney, it's been years since the last good, soaking rain. In the wintertime, thick clouds hover over the Wyoming Range, then vanish, with no trace of snow left to show they were ever there. The hillsides have lost the tint of green that lingers through winter. In its place is a dull gray hue, the color of gunpowder. The surface of meadows that should be lush with timothy and redtop are cracked, and dust rises up from the horses' hooves. Where the creek crosses the road, the water barely trickles between rocks that once created rapids.

The cattle left here in August. In a "normal" year, they wouldn't be out of the mountains yet, but this year, they didn't go to the mountains because there was no feed. Two full months of gain were lost to the drought, two months in which cattle harden, and calves begin to grow fat. Some of the cattle went to the Sandhills of Nebraska. It was a good year in the Sandhills.

The rancher had hoped to make about sixty bucks a head on this bunch of cattle; instead, he'll lose thirty.

The neighbor's cattle are leaving today. All of them. The owner hopes to find cornstalks and wheat stubble for them to graze through the winter, and while it will cost more than to bring hay to the cows, there may not be snow this winter, or rain in the spring. He's not sure what to do about calving yet, but if there's no feed at home, he'll find a way to make it work, a way that will mean the difference between making a profit and maybe breaking even.

There's a fair amount of grass left on Middle Piney. Back in the willows, the beavers have done a good job of holding what little water the mountains offer, and green meadows abound that can't be seen from the road. Willows are slowly creeping into the bitterbrush, and the creek provides a haven for cutthroats and brookies. Sandhill cranes hatched this summer test their awkward wings, and they will fly soon. When cold and hunters move them out of the higher mountains, moose will move in to work on the willow and aspen. Elk will come later, and there will be grass left for them. There is cover for the deer, and water for the muskrats.

One rancher could have kept his steers and heifers another month, maybe more. Another could still turn cows and calves down on the creek and let them grub grass and sedges, and maybe, even some of the willow and aspen. From a purely financial sense, it would work for another year, and winter may bring enough snow to lend a shimmer of light to the drought.

The owner of the cows is philosophical about that.

"If we get the kind of winter we need," he says, "those cows'll be glad they're gone, and by God, I will be too."

The choice was up to these ranchers, and no one else. Like the ranchers on Shell Creek, these men and their families chose to care for the land first, to take a certain loss in the face of potential gain. As some choose to leave the swamp, others choose to leave the grass and willows, to adjust their own desires and wishes. Ranchers make these choices every day. For those who have survived generations, for those who will be there when it finally rains, the choice is not difficult.

Some fail to hear the voice of the land. They will not last. But, the land will survive. In the land lies strength, and resilience.

And, from the land will come more ranchers.

BUYING BULLS

I guess it never occurred to me that this day might happen, that I would be wandering around the sale barn, shooting the shit, and harassing small children, waiting for my son Joe to look over the sale catalog one more time. He was out of junior college, managing a small ranch in the mountains near Dubois, and this was his show, not mine.

Joe was sitting at a table, careful not to get his elbow in a blob of spilled barbecue sauce, hat tilted to the side, studying their genetics, talking with the other folks from the ranch, rubbing his head.

I always hated buying bulls, and I never really knew why. Growing up on a ranch that sold bulls, you would think it would be a cakewalk, but buying bulls was pure agony. I spent hours looking over the catalogs, devouring the potential and downside of each bull, sorting cattle on a piece of paper, getting them down to the handful I wanted. Wheat from chaff. Iron from ore. Oxide from rust.

The agony was in the waiting, I thought as I watched him talk with his crew. They had a handful of bulls they really wanted, and another handful they might be interested in, if the price was right. They had a budget. There was a number they could live with, and if things were good, they could buy the best. If not, they might go home with an empty trailer.

He had asked me if they should bring the trailer, and I'd said no. Don't get your hopes up. If you drag the trailer, you might feel obligated to have something in it when you go home. Stick to your plan. See what happens. This is a business deal. Know what bulls you want before you sit down. Look them over in the pen, but don't look past the numbers. Stick to your guns. Don't panic when the ones you want sell high. You should really worry if the ones you want sell cheap.

I didn't even have a buyer number, and I could already feel tightness in my chest.

Claudine Gardner was suddenly next to me, like she had appeared out of the ether, and she laughed again about the "boys."

"My God," she shook her head, "they were just babies."

She pointed out her great-grandchildren, sitting in the stands, waiting for the sale, and I shook my head.

"You aren't that old, Claudine," I smiled, and she laughed.

Claudine and her husband, Dave, were the best partners we could have had at Red Canyon when we started out. Some of their kids were close to my age then, and some of their grand-kids were little then, like that son of mine who was studying the bull sale catalog now.

"Where does the time go?" Claudine asked, and I stared at my son.

Given the right moment, I would have made some cynical comment about time, about the fact that we need to understand that our children are meant to grow up, and we are meant to grow older. I might have made light of the question, and reminded her that we weren't growing older, only smarter. As it was, I had absolutely nothing to say.

"Are you still cooking at the sale barn?" I asked, and she laughed, the same gusto in her voice I had always remembered.

"Oh, hell yes!" she said, and I wondered how many meals she had cooked, how many people she had talked to, and how many more would be in the mix. I walked my mind through the lunch line one more time, and realized she was the only one who had been there when I came to the first bull sale in that barn. What was that? Twenty years ago? Holy hell, more like thirty.

"It's fun to see those boys grow up," she grinned.

I wasn't so sure. I was still thinking of "those boys" as the boys they once were, not as men who were buying bulls, pitting their dollars against others who wanted the bulls equally and had more money to put on the table.

There was more in my mind than bulls and barbecue sauce, but it was all mixed together now.

This was my oldest son, Joe, the one who wanted nothing to do with cattle, or horses, or country. This was the son who said he would be a pilot, an architect, an artist. What the hell was happening here?

He was asking me a question, poking his finger at the catalog, at numbers and words too small for me to read without a pair of cheaters. I fished them out of my coat pocket and looked at the list. Eight bulls.

From a yard full of nearly sixty prospects, he had narrowed the list to eight, and as I looked at their numbers and remembered them from the pens outside, he had picked a set of bulls that were outstanding.

"You may not get three out of those eight," I warned. "Hell, you may not get any."

"Well," he smiled, "you told me not to bring the trailer."

The hum and rhythm of an auction began behind me, and Joe wandered over to the stands and sat down. The first bull he had his sights on was tenth on the list. It was one hell of a prospect, light birth weight, great growth potential, a bull raised at high elevation, out of one of the top bulls in the breed. He was perfect for what they hoped to do with their cow herd.

After the first bull sold, Joe was back.

"Where do you sit?" he asked, and I laughed. I never sat at a bull sale in my life. Sitting doesn't fit me well when I'm relaxed, and it sure as hell doesn't work when you're nervous. I told him I stood in the alley between the stands, where I could walk around, pace like a new father, and spit. It always seemed kind of crazy to sit there like I would see something I missed in the pens, or that maybe the bull would give me a wink. If I sat in the stands, I would twist myself into a worse knot than I would when the boys were wrestling, and I sure as hell never sat at any of those either.

We stood together and watched the next seven bulls sell, some high, some moderate, none in his price range, and I could feel the panic rising in my chest. The ninth bull was in the ring, and the bidding started a good $500 out of his range. His bull was up.

At $2,000, the ringman caught a bid and the game was on. Joe got in at $2,250 and no sooner than one bid-taker hollered "yes!" another was howling like a coyote. The first bull he wanted went by in a cloud of cash and a scatter of wood chips thrown by cloven hooves. He wasn't even in the game on that one.

Joe looked at his sale catalog and shook his head. He looked at the catalog again and began to turn the pages. One of his eight was gone, for nearly double the money he had to spend. The next bull, a half-brother to his selection, sold for high dollar, and he was looking for something, *anything*, to buy. What the hell? He had a buyer number, and he ate the free lunch, and they had bulls to sell, and he needed bulls. It was clear as sunlight he wanted the same thing everyone else wanted. But, he didn't have his trailer hitched to the truck.

After he had nearly worn out the pages of the catalog, he turned around and looked at me. A grin worked its way across his face, and he shook his head.

"This really sucks," he sighed. "I thought it would be more fun."

"Howdy, Parson. Welcome to hell," I said in my best Lee Marvin drawl, the line blatantly stolen from Ben Rumson in *Paint Your Wagon*, the same line the kids had heard all their lives.

Joe sat down, and we talked about what he wanted to do with the cows at the ranch. He had an incredible grasp of genetics and economics. That, he had gotten from college. He gave me the background genetics on the bulls he wanted, and that, he got from research and study of livestock. He talked about the type of cows he wanted—good mothers, feminine daughters, calm cattle, comfortable cattle. He was looking for bulls that fit his image of the herd, not his image of himself. He was actually fitting his vision of cattle to the landscape he lived in, including the people he lived with.

"I got that part from you," he said, and he wandered back between the bleachers.

I was stunned, to the point of immobility. Only occasionally in our lives had I seen some recognition that something I said had taken hold, and now, one score and one year later, my son said he had learned something from me. It wasn't a moment of truth, but one of enlightenment, and the enlightenment was not for him. It was for me.

He bought the next bull he wanted, right at his limit, and the bid-taker looked at him with an air of skepticism. Who the hell was this young pup bidding on good bulls before he could shave on a daily basis? Was this a joke? The ringman wagged his fingers. Joe fumbled through his catalog, looking for his buyer number. The sale slowed down, and everyone in the barn looked into the alley between the stands.

"Two-forty-nine!" the bid-taker yelled.

"Two-forty-nine!" the auctioneer repeated, and he ramped up his "hooda hooda hooda" rhythm and offered another bull.

"Who the hell is that kid?" some old man behind me asked his friend.

"That kid," I told him, "is my son."

Joe got his second bull, and his third, and I drank a lot of coffee, and talked to a lot of old ladies and old men while he did his job. I went over to help him settle the bill, but the women at the table gave me the motherly eye, and I had more coffee.

We rode home in his ranch truck, him driving, me riding shotgun. His brother and the ranch crew sat in the back seat and chattered, and I stared at the scenery.

"You did really well," I said.

"I've never been that nervous in my life," he sighed.

If only he knew, I thought. If only he knew.

MANAGING FOR SUSTAINABILITY

Much has been made of the term "sustainability" of late. From Wall Street to the back forty, we surround ourselves in sustainability jargon, often without asking what exactly is meant by the term. A quick survey of five collegiate texts on ecology finds none with the term either defined or used. One text made passing reference to a "sustainable-earth worldview" in separating "neo-Malthusians" from "cornucopians," but the word "sustainability" is not found in any of those sampled. Falling back to *Merriam-Webster's Dictionary*, "sustainability" is determined to mean "to keep in existence; to maintain."

In the natural world, we know very few things absolutely, but one thing we must understand is that disturbance and change is the norm, and not the exception. In the longer term, change may be subtle—a cut bank along Red Canyon Creek is a trip through geologic time—layers of silt, then layers of ancient plants, repeated again and again. To the casual observer, it is just another concave bank above a meandering stream. Geologists go berserk.

"I'm not sure what we're seeing here," the geologists told me. "I think it could be residue from some of the major glaciations, piled up over periods of relative calm. Bottom line, the top layers are probably at least 100,000 years old."

Disturbance may be on a massive geologic scale, such as that delved out by earthquakes or volcanic activity, or on a more moderate scale, such as changes brought about by fire, flood, hurricane, or drought. On a more localized scale, short-term influences from herbivory, parasites, and disease may also alter the existing condition.

Sustainability cannot be defined as a force to maintain the present ecological, economic, or social structure. Instead, managing for sustainability implies embracing change, adapting to those changes, and predicting future directions for natural systems. Unlike some of the harder sciences, like mathematics, physics, and chemistry, the only rules in ecology revolve around what we will learn next.

Natural resource management is the art of blending ecology, economy, and culture into an output that will meet sustainability tests in all three areas, and generally, all at the same time. The history of most cultures shows that we tend to race off in one direction or another, only to find ourselves limited by one of these three. In the late 1800s in the United States, citizens were encouraged by a benevolent government to settle the West. Those who managed to get there could lay title to 160 acres of "prime" land, settle, and meet the Jeffersonian standards of a "gentleman."

This concept was both culturally and economically sound, but it failed to recognize that soils, vegetation, and climate of the "new" western frontier were as different from the same conditions in the "old" western frontier. Illinois and Kentucky, once termed wilderness, were a far cry from the paper-thin soils of Wyoming, Idaho, and Nevada. And, while 160 acres of prime land in the midsection of the nation would support a family, the same acreage west of the 100th meridian would barely support a family of marmots.

In China, maximization of both farming and logging, beginning in the 1940s and 1950s, ultimately led to the realization that watersheds were being altered so radically that they may all end up as an extension of the nation by being carried to the Pacific Ocean. The solution in many cases was issuance of a "logging ban," or a "grazing ban," or a "fire ban," or a combination of all three. Huge public works projects went so far as to plant trees, install drip irrigation systems, and demand compliance from people and plants alike. Most failed, not because they weren't ecologically based, but because starving people don't listen well to environmental resolution that fails to include an economic future.

Finally, there are countless examples of models that were sound ecologically and economically but failed to meet cultural standards. In India, poverty is rampant, despite the fact that the country is among the world leaders in cattle production. Many experts have pointed out the fact that use of those animals as food would not only bring economic rewards but also remove some of the ecological pressures from an overabundance of grazing animals. The Hindu faith remains unmoved by such logic. In another case, in South America, time and energy went into teaching villagers to diversify income sources from cattle to aquaculture, tourism, and other endeavors, with the understanding that such prosperity would ease pressures to convert rain forest to pasture. In the end, with the added wealth at hand, villagers did what they had always done to show prosperity—they bought more cattle! Of the three fundamental components of sustainability, culture will nearly always be the most powerful.

At Red Canyon Ranch, our challenge was to enhance and maintain the diversity of biological resources, increase the economic output, and allow for enjoyment of the landscape, within the bounds of what society would tolerate. For example, a number of advisors insisted that raising bison would be the most ecologically and economically sound path to follow. But, none of the local ranchers raised bison, and only one had any interest whatsoever in considering raising bison. If we hoped to learn from the project in a meaningful way, we had to do so within the general norms of the livestock industry locally. Once that was determined, it was time to begin the process of management.

From the outset, it was understood that the landscape was "owned" by a variety of interests. Most of the ranch is public land, divided fairly equally between the US Forest Service and the Bureau of Land Management (BLM). A county road slices through the heart of the deeded land. At the time, Roy Packer called the shots on the BLM, and Brad Russell had the final word on the Forest Service. Wyoming Game and Fish set seasons and harvest objectives for wildlife and issued licenses to hunt on most of the ranch. The state engineer controlled the water rights. Local hunters and fishermen had their own "spot" on the landscape. And, nearly every one of those people had more background and information on the ranch than the owner or the manager.

The first requirement was development of a goal that defined outcomes, and the process that would lead to those benchmarks. It was imperative that the goal was inclusive of all landowners, including neighbors. It was equally vital that the goal recognized the knowledge, freely given, from those who knew the landscape best. When we were able to look at the landscape together, rather than only our own portions of the whole, we were able to make better decisions. We also found incredible flexibility in management.

There is an old story about a young man being presented with a jar by his mentor, and on the table in front of him, an array of large rocks, gravel, and sand. The mentor tells the young man to fill the jar, without leaving any of the material on the table. "It will all fit," he is told, and he is left alone. Ultimately, what he learns is that it will only fit if the big rocks are put in first, followed by the gravel, and finally, the sand, which will fill the spaces left by the larger material. In managing land, you must first begin with the big rocks.

All landscapes are defined by their geology. Terrain, parent material for soils, site potential for vegetation, and habitat niches are driven by geologic influences. Included within this is the hydrologic regime, much of which is invisible to our daily inspections. Understanding the geology first will help us avoid selection of management options that are ill-fitted to the local situation. For example, one group of students challenged me by insisting that erosion was one of the key "problems" to be solved, until they stood back and looked up at the top of the canyon walls and realized that erosion instead defined the setting in which to work. Further investigation by Dennis Dahms, a geologist from Georgia State University, confirmed relic portions of at least seven sets of terraces, each at a different elevation and time, each left by a distinct major geologic event.

Second, we have to understand the natural range of variability that defined the watershed. Historic precipitation amounts are a key, but more importantly, historic patterns of precipitation help explain the vegetation we now see on the ground. Likewise, herbivory and fire influences can help guide decision-making on the ground. In central Wyoming, we know that large herbivores played an essential role in influencing vegetation, and insect outbreaks likely had a much larger effect in some years. Fire occurred on a large scale, at intervals of about 100 years in lodgepole pine and Douglas fir, and it is also believed that smaller-scale fire was a regular influence. Drought was common, though patterns of climate change may be altering the normal range of variability today. While there is much we do not know about the natural range of variability, we can begin to focus decision-making by using the things we do know and testing other assumptions we may choose.

The working assumptions are that the area was heavily used by elk, bighorn sheep, deer, and pronghorn. These animals responded to a variety of annual cues. Beginning in the spring, animals followed riparian corridors from lower wintering areas. As feed on winter ranges diminished, stream corridors tended to "green up," attracting herds of ungulates. As snowpacks receded, the line of lush forage moved higher in elevation, and temperatures began to warm. Ultimately, many of these herds ended the summer at the highest elevations, where forage quality was highest, nights were cool, and insects were less of a pest. In the fall, many of these patterns were reversed. Plants also tell this story. The first plants to produce along the riparian areas are generally grasses and forbs, while woody species like willow, dogwood, and birch leaf out later. It can be assumed this is a plant strategy to avoid herbivory, and a management indicator of when best to use those areas for grazing. Two things cannot be assumed—that these areas were managed by wild ungulates, or that they were not grazed.

Ultimately, most of us in the West live in ecosystems that were characterized by a constant state of disturbance, and massive shifts in weather patterns and other nonbiological conditions. The norm was abnormality. There was, and is, no "average" year. Even with solid experimental design to address control, constant, and baseline conditions, we simply cannot account for time and space in natural systems. We are attempting to place our incredibly short human lifespan at a higher level of importance than geologic time, ecological phenomena like 200-year droughts, or shorter-term evolutionary forces. It may work in our own lifetimes, but it will not work in the longer term. If we hope to maintain stability in natural systems, we will have to learn to embrace and understand chaos and instability.

Rain does not follow the plow, though it once appeared to do so. God may provide, but we don't know exactly what it is that God will provide. Nature may reach equilibrium in the absence of management, but that equilibrium will not always look like pictures in a coffee-table book. And beware the notion that we have systems that are either "unmanaged," or "pristine." Humans have had a profound effect on ecosystems for our entire existence, not just for the period upon which we can blithely blame our parents and thus absolve ourselves of responsibility.

So, how should we approach management of natural systems? First and foremost, we need to understand that four basic processes guide and direct everything we do on the ground. We learn these in elementary school, in middle school, in college, and then forget them completely when we set out to manage land. The four processes are the water cycle, nutrient cycle, energy flow, and vegetative dynamics. No matter what we might choose to do in a natural environment, we should be focused on one of these four components, though most often, we will find ourselves working on two or more in the end. If we are restoring a wetland that has dried up, for instance, we should be focused on the water cycle. Without a properly functioning hydrologic regime, we cannot hope to move plant succession, or conduct energy. Nor can we expect the anaerobic processes normal in a functioning wetland to exist. In other systems, we may find the limiting process to be energy flow, often overlooked because we simply don't have the mental capacity to easily understand things we cannot see. Current models of stable states, transitions, and triggers often lead us to the conclusion that plant succession is the problem, though that may simply be an indication that one of the other processes (such as energy flow or nutrient cycling) has failed. Which of these is the key to moving a system in the direction desired?

The word "desired" is purposely chosen, and not from a thesaurus. Human desires drive all decisions, and some of our desires are insane. We all want home to smell like freshly baked bread when we visit, not stinky socks. We sometimes insist upon one without the other, failing to remember you have to take the good with some bad. For forests in our part of the world to remain green and lush, they need to turn black once in a while. For a single species to evolve successfully, some individuals need to die, whether from disease that develops immunity in the survivors, or predation that alters behavior.

Whether we choose a hands-off approach, or more active engagement with the resource, we have only a handful of tools we can apply to the resource. Those tools are fire, grazing animals, rest, other organisms, and technology. As an example, irrigation is a tool of technology, used to impact the water cycle, leading to a change in the plant community. Using the same example, chemical fertilizers are a technological treatment that may increase yields, while enhancing soil fertility through close attention to bacteria and organic matter in the soil itself would be management through other organisms.

Unfortunately, we seem to be hopelessly addicted to technology. Using the example of a streambank scoured by spring runoff, countless groups have been asked what they would do about the situation. They would get out their GPS unit and lock in the coordinates, then hustle back to the office to lay out the area on ArcView, and enhance the image to lay it out in CAD. Once done with that, they are quick to select a D-9 Cat with a ripper blade to slope the banks to the angle of repose, add a layer of erosion cloth and hydroseed with a mulch. Inside the stream, they design riprap along the scoured bank, add tree revetments, rock barbs, and other structures above and below to control the flow of the stream.

The scouring is natural. The area is smaller than a pickup truck. In time, the soil taken from that bank will build numerous bars below the cut, and willows and other vegetation will occupy those sites, stabilizing the stream. For thousands of years, the stream has worked this way, and it will continue to do so for thousands more.

At the same time we feed our addiction to technology, we ignore the most powerful tools at our disposal. It is somewhat compelling to think that we spent most of the past century trying to eliminate fire in nearly every landscape, and at least half of the century trying to eliminate domestic grazing animals. That would leave us rest, technology, and other organisms, many of which we have also tried to purge. We are attempting to solve incredibly complex riddles with only half our brain. Instead, we need to place the tools in context of the landscape and apply them in a manner that will lead us toward our desired outcome. By controlling the time of year grazing occurs, we can have significant effects on plant communities, and production. Different stocking rates and densities will lead to variable outcomes. The same is true with fire. We can do more, faster, using the tools under which the ecosystem evolved than we can by locking it up and hoping for the best.

Monitoring is an essential component to successful management. While many desire hard numbers and replication, that will not always be possible. Photos and observation are essential factors in good monitoring. Livestock production records are valuable. For the past ten years, it has become apparent to me that much of what we seek to know can be aggregated into sampling of fish and birds. Together, they offer a very clear picture of how systems are responding to management. Everything that happens in a watershed ends up in the stream and adjacent riparian areas, and those areas are rich in animal life. Diversity of bird species, and the presence of indicator species offer a clear picture of how the system is functioning. Likewise, fisheries aggregate water quality, insect production, water temperature, stream characteristics, and other factors that can be used to evaluate the health of the overall system. It is important to select meaningful parameters that will be monitored, and to do the monitoring on a regular schedule.

In conclusion, managing for sustainability relies on having a solid understanding of the ecosystems in which we work, and the forces that led us to where we find ourselves today. Using that understanding, we can develop management models and reasonable expectations for what the system will look like, and the steps it will follow to get there—goals and benchmarks. If we identify the process we are attempting to affect, we can select the tools that will lead us in the desired direction. And always, we monitor, and examine outcomes to see if we are indeed making the progress we anticipate.

Finally, we must understand that it has taken millions of years to get us where we are. Oftentimes, the management we apply will take decades to show results, and it seems that we wait, wait, and wait, only to see the change occur in a matter of months. In *The Education of Little Tree*, a young Indian boy pesters his grandfather with wonderfully intricate and elegant questions, only to be told it is "the way."

Sometimes that is indeed the best answer.

THE TEST

In life, in education, in business—success will *always* come down to other people. Your ability to embrace other ideas, other cultures, and other opinions will have a greater bearing on your future than anything else you can learn or do.

My wife has a saying taped to her computer that says, "People will forget what you say. They will forget what you do. But they will NEVER forget how you made them feel."

Every day, no matter where you are, do what you can to make the place you a live a better community. Pass a beer over the fence. Share your barbecue. Rescue the neighbor's cat. Put some money in the pot at the grocery store. Tease a little kid.

Ask yourself once in a while if what you are doing is making you a better person, or just making you better than someone else.

You know the difference between right and wrong. Don't act like you don't get it. That white crown on the top of chicken crap is still chicken crap.

"There but for the grace of God go I." My brother and I once made fun of someone far less blessed, and my father said those nine words. I have never forgotten it. And every time I see someone who is challenged in ways I cannot imagine, I find myself asking if I really have the courage it takes to do what they do. Don't act tough unless you are. If you really are tough, you don't have to act at all.

Mine the wisdom of older people. Sometimes, a simple question to an old warhorse will lead you to things you could not imagine. I once asked an old woman in China where she lived and was shown a real world few will ever see. I've had the same experiences in Colorado, and Mexico, and Africa, and in my own hometown. Respect for your elders will be returned to you many times over, usually when you need it most.

Give your spare change to people who have to beg for it, even just a little bit. I gave sixty cents to a man in St. Louis, and he laughed at me. I gave fifty cents to a woman in Memphis, and she gave me a hug. I probably wasted the sixty cents, but you never know. I'm willing to bet somebody ate at White Castle in Memphis. I gave two bucks to a guy in Boulder, and he used it for gas in his BMW. He'll have to live with that.

The smartest and most important thing I have done in my life is to marry my wife, Lynn. I have had to find courage, humility, and grace. I've had to learn about women's sizes, why I can live with five pairs of shoes and she with no less than sixty. But I also have the most incredible joy and love, which I will guarantee you is stronger than anything else you will ever experience.

We have three wonderful children, and I can only tell you that when you choose to be a mother or father, you should place that role above all others. If you have children, make that your priority. If you want to leave a legacy, love your children enough to be there when they need you.

Follow your heart. Crying at sappy movies is good exercise for your emotional side. Some only find their heart when it is operated upon.

Some people worry about the next generation. I could not be more excited about the next generation in natural resources—which is YOU. If us old guys are smart enough to let you think and act, and you are brave enough to ask us how the hell we got here, things can only get better. I can't wait until you start telling me why I'm wrong. There's nothing I like better than a good argument.

Someday, that girl you thought was too fat, or the boy you thought was too small, will grow up and you will wish like heck you had kept your mouth shut.

If you're going to speak up, and you should, learn to savor the taste of crow. You'll eat less and less of it as you go along, but by the time you get the flavor down, you will be more honest, and more tactful.

Celebrate failure. Make some mistakes. If you make it to next year without screwing up, you simply aren't trying hard enough. If you think you can live with being average, think again.

We learn from falling down and getting back up. We get smarter, and we learn to try again. Just don't get addicted to failure.

My sons wrestle, the most agonizing thing a child can do to their parents. The motto of the Ron Thon Memorial tournament . . . "Win with humility, lose with dignity," says a lot. On either end of that spectrum in life, whether winning or losing, make sure it ends with humility and dignity. There is nothing quite so hollow as winning when there is no other option.

Do something good for someone else every day of your life. It can be something simple, like opening a door, picking up a bag of groceries, or just smiling. Work really hard on this one—let it be instinctive. It might be the most important thing of all.

Learn to hug each other. It seems to be a lost art. None of us are above a hug, and most of us miss them. Most of our lives started with hugs, and most end with them. Why waste the best part of life without something so meaningful? And, when you hug someone, mean it. Anyone can tell a fake hug.

Don't lie. It just complicates life. Always tell the truth. You will never regret this decision.

Talk to the person in the seat next to you on airplanes, or buses, or a bench. Ask people what they do. You will be amazed at what you can learn in an hour, and you will be amazed at where it will lead. Open yourself to other people. Sometimes you will regret this, but mostly, you will find your life rewarded and your mind expanded.

Listen to rock and roll before breakfast. I highly recommend "Lunatic Fringe" by Red Ryder, and anything by AC/DC. It is amazing how this will enhance your day.

Fall hopelessly in love sometime. Even if it doesn't work out, it really is worth it.

It is a small world. Never forget that. When you find yourself hanging from a strand of grass on the edge of a cliff, the person on top will be someone you know. How would you like them to remember you?

Have faith, wherever you choose to find it. There are many things beyond your control or understanding. Sometimes, as in *The Education of Little Tree*, it is just "the way." Believe in yourself and have faith that life is good.

Take a nap every chance you get.

Every day you rise and suck air is a gift. Don't waste a single day in anger or despair. How you feel is up to you. How you make others feel is also up to you.

You have chosen a profession that is not known for creating fortunes. Instead, you will find great joy in simple things, like a family of otters, a chinook, or a salamander. You will smile at green grass, the smell of a skunk, the reality of cold wind and gentle sunshine, your ability to taste water. These are incredible things, and the people you meet in your life will be very, very special. And, you can wear jeans almost every day.

The most relevant quote about work in natural resources comes from F. Scott Fitzgerald. He said, "The test of a first-rate intelligence is the ability to hold two opposed ideas in the mind at the same time, and still retain the ability to function." Such is the path you've chosen. Thank you for making our world better.

Finally, take a moment and look around this room. Lock your eyes with someone who has been especially helpful in your education. For many of you, it will be the parents who are here to see you attain this milestone. For some it will be a boyfriend, girlfriend, or spouse. For others, there will be a professor who made it all make sense. No matter how many, or whom, I challenge you to make their day in the next twenty-four hours by thanking them for getting you here.

Say the words, "I love you." Often.

After this day, the rest of your life will come down to how you work with people, and how you choose to be as a person. I hope you choose to be a person of grace, charity, integrity, humor, honesty, and above all, passion. Be what you are, for today, you are mighty, full of energy, and utterly spectacular. Every tomorrow should be nothing less. NEVER forget that.

COMMON SENSE

There are a lot of wise people in the world, and I've been privileged to have the ear and counsel of many. Some had no more than a clean shirt and their integrity; others accumulated great fortune and kept their integrity. None were quick to offer judgment, though most were free with their wisdom, meted out in measured amounts and intensity. Sometimes harsh as a spring storm, more often calm as a mountain pool, each of them offered something different from the others. But, all agreed on a single most important trait, or measure of wisdom.

They called it common sense.

Not one of the wise people I have known disdained science. They valued science for its ability to help them understand *why* things happen. None scoffed at economic theory, choosing instead to use economics as a tool to predict what might come of a particular action. Statistics offered some means of predicting the value of an investment, or of assessing the results of a chosen path. Together, use of those disciplines and others gave measurement of success or failure, a manner of evaluating risk, and when applied with common sense, sustainability.

Ten years ago, environmental assessment was reduced from a broad *feel* for the land to a nearly microscopic scale. Instead of looking at the overall impact of actions, science led us away from common sense. Overreliance on "models" led to supposed results that could not be sustained in reality. There was no feel for the integrated relationships on ranches, or in local communities. Broad-based ecologists were replaced with a corps of biologists—"specialists." Instead of integrating the knowledge of specialists and building wisdom with common sense, environmental "awareness" created thousands of little paradigms, and a climate for internal battles between specialists. Many of those are still operative.

For years, landowners and land managers have struggled to gain an understanding of how to integrate these values and realities. More recently, watershed approaches to problem solving have led us to look at the environment on a broader scale. Whether applied to business or ecology, the true measure of wisdom still lies in our ability to integrate what we know into actions that will lead to desired conditions. Maybe common sense has found a place in environmental management. Maybe we can combine common sense with science, and look for solutions, rather than pointing our fingers at "problems."

That is the intent behind programs like holistic resource management, ecosystem management, and even assessments of biodiversity. The ranching industry has been largely supportive of the concepts of a broad overview of natural systems, especially when integrated with economic realities and cultural, quality-of-life goals.

It has taken years of effort to understand and integrate thinking at a localized watershed scale, to involve landowners and others in management for sustainability. It has taken years to gain an understanding for the subtle differences that make stream systems behave and react differently. It will take even more years to gain understanding for the dynamics of rangelands, or forests, or alpine communities. We remain in an embryonic stage of understanding, but the human need to be informed has evolved light years.

The results are overwhelming. Ranch plans across the West allocate forage for wildlife, not as an afterthought, but as a vital component of management. Water quality and quantity are integrated into business plans, as are long-term vegetative goals. Ranchers throughout the West are developing fisheries, reintroducing and managing beavers, using fire as a management tool, taking steps to increase biodiversity—to protect and enhance wetlands and riparian areas. And, while some may choose to avoid reality and argue the degree and rate of change, the land is responding.

The ranching industry has changed.

In many cases, it has taken an effort to un-remember the last set of guidelines for management. Only fifteen years ago, the ranchers were being paid to drain wetlands and burn willows. The major thrust in riparian management was getting rid of plants that used water. In other cases, change has

meant learning new things, but the ranching industry has always been willing to learn and try new things. The bottom line to successful ranching operations is still open space and sustainability.

That is why the recent political announcements from the non-state of Washington, D.C., have raised such great anxiety in the country.

The principal weapons of partisan politics have become science, economics, and statistics, grossly misapplied. Rather than seeking common ground and ferreting out common-sense solutions on a watershed scale, or an integrated ranch scale, it is easy to follow a path that will lead away from logic, into a void of understanding. Recent advances in coordinated resource management . . . riparian and wetland enhancement . . . nonpoint source pollution abatement . . . sediment control . . . holistic resource management . . .

biological weed and pest control . . . ecosystem management . . . and above all, the willingness to openly involve people from different backgrounds in critical cultural and ecological decisions is much too valuable to lose.

The last thing the remaining pieces of natural country need right now is a "national standard" for environmental management. What we need are cowboys, broad-based ecologists, and resource managers, along with other folks who are willing to cast aside their political agendas. In every case where that has happened, the result has been profit for the landowner, and profit for the land.

The goal should be sustainability, and sustainability is grounded in the balance between ecology, economy, and culture. Getting there takes nothing more than common sense.

SAGEBRUSH AND SNOW

It was a fairly typical winter morning in southern Wyoming. The sun was bright white in a pale blue sky, the result of a low-pressure system that brought cold air and forty-mile-an-hour winds. The high-pressure system that left the state two days earlier dumped ten inches of fluffy snow over the landscape, and some of that snow blew into miniature dunes behind each rock and bush. Today, most of the snow went airborne three feet off the ground, high enough to miss the rocks and brush that could hold it in place. The temperature hovered around zero.

Somewhere near Dana Ridge, amidst a bizarre mixture of sunshine, fog, and swirling snow, a herd of antelope moved along a narrow spit of land, pushed north by the hard south wind. They walked single file, heads down, and they moved slowly. For those in front, each step was a process; their hooves settled onto hard, drifted snow, broke through, then found the ground beneath. Every step was a new adventure, like blind men walking on thawing ice. The antelope behind found easier going, just as geese in formation draft those in front. Unlike geese, the antelope never changed position. One followed the other, ears to butt, butt to ears, noses to the ground.

Had it been late winter, it would have been a death march. More than one winter has taken whole herds of antelope in the end, but this was early winter, and the next change in the weather would bring melting snow, open country, and adequate browse.

In that swirl of ice and agony were three colors. The sky was blue. The snow was white, and everything else was a light shade of brown.

I tried to count the antelope on the high ground—a hundred or so—and followed their path both forward and behind. Even with the wind, their trail from the south was obvious. In their wake, they left a drifted line that had been drawn for thousands of years. More than likely, on a summer day, you could follow that same line in either direction on a trail pounded into the landscape by millions of footsteps. Blowing snow clears ridges and fills valleys. When you're moving, you suck it up, take the wind on your ass, and follow high ground. Find a warm place. Ride it out.

Then I saw the rest of the antelope. There were at least four hundred of them huddled into an area not much bigger than a football field, on the lee side of the rim. Above them, sandstone rocks created an overhang about twelve inches wide. Beneath them was bare ground. Snow swirled over their heads in a fog and built a drift to the west. Between them, sagebrush stood no more than two feet high, but each bush was tipped with a seasonal change of color, and that color was a light shade of brown.

The sagebrush plant is an incredible species, evergreen and deciduous at once. It is a rare plant that sends a long, deep-drinking tap root, and at the same time, short, shallow adventitious roots that can take advantage of rains that barely penetrate the soil. The color of the spice is pale green. Ask anyone who has lived in the sagebrush steppe, and they will tell you, sagebrush has a blue-green hue. Five hundred antelope in the lee side of ridge convinced me that sagebrush is a light shade of brown.

Suddenly, I understood the color of antelope.

It wasn't a revelation, really. Nor was it the answer to a plaguing question. It was just a blast of reality. Something that never made sense was suddenly clear. Question and answer appeared at the same time.

It is easy to understand the bright red color of a calf moose when you are deep in the willows where they are born. The gray color of mule deer and sage grouse are almost a dead-on match for sagebrush. Bighorn sheep can lie down on a rock and disappear. Elk can hide in dark timber, aspens, or shadows. Predators are no different. The stripes of tigers blend into grass. The spots of bobcats dissolve in trees. Polar bears never leave a place that is covered in ice.

Antelope live in a world of lustrous and pale greens, but they only disappear in winter. Antelope are susceptible one season of the year, the only time speed and keen eyes are of little help. In that season, the blue greens of sagebrush and the verdant colors of prairie grass are gone, and the plains turn into a jigsaw puzzle of stark whites and tans. The growth at the top of sagebrush plants turns the color of an antelope, and when the wind howls, no other colors catch the eye.

Antelope can crowd into a draw and hide for days on end. The wind erases track and scent, and for miles and miles, antelope look like sagebrush and snow. For thousands of years, this has been their way of survival at the time they are most vulnerable. For longer than we have been here, this has worked for antelope, and for what we can see, it will continue.

Very often, what we see is not what we understand. We take things for granted, and never ask why. We take what we see as the way things are and always were, and we never once ask ourselves if the colors of antelope might tell us something.

In the swirling snow on a winter's day, I realized that the landscape in front of me, a barren expanse of withered western wheatgrass, sagebrush, sand, and nothing fancy was just right for an antelope.

Sometimes, nothing is everything.

EYES ON FIRE

J ake is somewhere on the mountain. Maybe in the bottom of the North Fork canyon. He might be on a timbered ridge behind Shoshone Lake. Could be in the sagebrush above Dickinson Park. Somewhere on the mountain.

He left five days ago in the darkness of early morning. It felt more like fall than summer. He went off in the direction of smoke. Kissed his mother and gave her a hug. Grinned a crooked smile. His White's boots rattled on the front step, and he was gone.

Since that moment, every rattle of a chopper blade catches his mother's ear. She feels each breeze, and comments on the speed and direction of the wind. She catches the nuances of fire burning in timber, brush, or grass. Her hazel eyes look constantly to the west, as if she might part the smoky haze and see her son.

Jake is nineteen years old, and harder than the knots in a fire-scarred ponderosa pine. His mother stares at his senior picture, and allows that he has gotten taller, his neck thicker, face leaner. She is torn between her need to nurture, and his need to take flight.

Lynn is conflicted by fire. She is not alone.

On the mountain, Jake is part of a close-knit crew, every one of them strong, competitive, and fearless. They give each other names like "Danger" and "Bad Ass" and "Torch." They work shoulder-to-shoulder in a world of soot and grime. They are trained to follow orders, to watch out for themselves and their partners. They will march into hell as a team. They will die for each other. Some do.

There is a fraternity of fire, a strange and powerful bond between men and women who wait for flames. Their world is a schizophrenia of love and hate for fire. These are people who see every thunderstorm for lightning, while everyone else prays for rain. They comprehend the natural world in its most visceral sense. In order to fight fire, you have to understand fire, and fear it greatly.

The conflagration is divine, for within this maelstrom swirl all the emotions of humankind. Fear triggers adrenaline. Epinephrine fires synapses and releases endorphins that calm the brain. Fire pay is nearly double regular pay. Complete exhaustion stimulates dreams. Sweat builds stamina. Crisis bonds men and women.

From our earliest learnings, we are taught that fire was essential to the evolution of our own species. Once discovered and harnessed, it was fire that shaped ecosystems, allowed advance into areas unknown, and allowed progression from the Stone Age to the Industrial Revolution. Fire was used as fuel, in battle, and as a means of manipulating wildlife so they might be taken as food.

Where did we lose our love of fire? How did we come to this place where one of our most important cultural and ecological forces fell from cherished ally to enemy?

We lost our love of fire when we sought to control fire. It is impossible to demand complete control from something you respect and admire, so fire was cloaked in shrouds of paganism, devil worship, and regressive behavior. A paradigm was built upon the shoulders of fire control, and agencies were constructed to resist ecological reality. While not the first extension of hubris, this may remain the most egregious display of human arrogance.

Worse, in the face of irrefutable evidence that fire was one of the most powerful forces in our natural world, we continued to deny that truth. Like the first lie, each misstep led to another, and another, until we had a hard time recognizing truth when it was in front of us.

Ostensibly, the rationale behind fire control was economic, protection of timber that could be hewn into homes, railroad ties, and entire towns. Trees unburned were trees that could be used. It is likely there was recognition of the fact that men with hand tools and balky mules could never beat back the power of nature. At first, fires close and visible got the bulk of attention. Even in hindsight, it is difficult to second-guess the logic behind the practice. People did what they believed was right.

Behind the wall of smoke that clouds the valley, Jake's hazel eyes are bloodshot. This day, people would not point out that he has his mother's eyes, as people have noted for his entire life. For five days, he has hacked the ground to mineral soil, building line to contain the fire. His meals have come from a box of surplus rations. He lies down with a hot wind and wakes with ice on his bivvy bag. Jake looks east, in the direction of his mother, hoping she isn't worried, knowing she is frantic. He smiles crookedly, a visage somewhere between joy and loathing.

Hidden beneath the war on fire was a vibrant logging economy. Hidden beneath that vibrant economy were houses built of sticks, emerging railroads that rested on wooden ties, and entire towns warmed by fireplaces, sometimes as many as a half dozen in a single home. Buried deep beneath the economy of wood lay the ecology of lodgepole pine forests that emerged as a mass of seedlings as thick as wool on a sheep and burned as intensely as gasoline every fifty or sixty years. Complete renewal. Complete removal.

But, not all fire works in the same manner. Plants have had millions of years to react to the stimuli around them, and some of their adaptations can be used to verify either the wisdom of a God, or the path of evolution, maybe even both. Ponderosa pines are elegantly suited to a world of fire, with long, fire-hardy trunks that eschew limbs at the lower levels—no sense leaving fuel below so flames can climb to the tops. As a result, grassland fires can run beneath the trees fairly often, remove competing seedlings, and rejuvenate the system on a regular basis.

Sagebrush ecosystems most likely evolved with thousands of lightning strikes, tens of thousands of grazing animals, and drought. Late season lightning had nothing to ignite in many cases, and in most others, found fuels wanting. The result was a series of small, patchy fires that created a patchwork of habitats within a sea of artemisia. Some creatures, like mountain plovers, found the most barren perfect for nesting. Others, like sage grouse, sought out areas unburned, ungrazed, and covered with shrubs to incubate their eggs. Life strategies varied, from camouflage, to speed, to sheer size, but the system was large, and varied enough to accommodate incredible diversity.

Still, the notion of destruction and chaotic reconstruction was anathema to humans. It remains that way today. We want to be in charge, make decisions, control outcomes. Politically, we posture and parry, and when we win a political battle, we assume we have won the war. But, lightning has no friends, and lightning has no enemies. When conditions are right, lightning and fuel copulate in a frenzy that creates potential for heaven or hell. Sometimes, as with children, it is a mixture of both.

"I never should have let him take that job," his mother said, green eyes facing the plume of midday smoke, as if her counsel would have made a difference. She quickly caught her own mistake and cried.

On the mountain, Jake found a fleeting cell signal and left a message for his mother.

"I'm fine," he said. Then there was a long pause.

"Don't worry," he added. Four words from Jake was a long chat.

Heaven and hell united. Lynn cried all night. The identical hazel eyes everyone always marveled about were the same again. This time, they were a world apart, and all were a bloodshot mess.

The fire raged for two more days and crept around like a thief for another week. Snow and rain and hand crews finally brought an end to the flames, and the fire beasts found their way off the mountain. Some flew out in helicopters. Some rode in massive engines, and some walked out the bottom of the canyons. Jake tromped into the house, hugged his mother, and stayed in the shower until the hot water was gone.

That fire season died right there. Six inches of snow were followed by warm fall rains. Grass tried to green again, and lightning vanished back into the clouds.

The warm fall moisture would lead to early growth of grasses in the spring, and those fine fuels would begin the cycle anew.

Fire was waiting, right around the corner.

I'LL GET THE GATE

There's a whole lot of blacktop across the West, and not much of it runs along survey lines. Most major highways wander along creek and river bottoms, just like those who headed west two centuries past, on foot, in wagons, pulling handcarts, or alternately floating and pulling boats. When we got smart enough to challenge the routes perfected by the Shoshone, Ute, Crow, and early explorers like Lewis and Clark, John Fremont, Jim Bridger, and John Wesley Powell, we drew nearly straight lines across the continent and forced our will first on the natural world, and then on travelers. Motels across Interstate 70, Interstate 80, and Interstate 90 do a thriving business in the winter. Little towns away from the double-lane artery wither, and sometimes die.

It isn't as simple as losing the grocery store or having to drive a long damn way to get lettuce that isn't brown. When Shawnee, Wyoming, finally succumbed to being off the main highway, the post office closed. Addresses changed, and mailboxes went away. It was declared that people could just "drive to town" to get their mail, even though town was fifty miles away. Local saloons and coffee shops went the same way, since many doubled as the postal stop, and pretty soon, the heart of the prairie was absorbed into the oversized gut of the nation.

Just as the heart of cities die as suburbia invades the country, the heart of the country dies as we lose small, even tiny, communities. With every little town that goes away, we lose a bit of heart, and a lot of soul.

I wasn't thinking those things when I left Douglas, Wyoming, one afternoon in the fall. I was tired of the racetrack interstate highway. I was sick of dodging trucks and campers and listening to bellyaching and whining, of noise that meant nothing. I was sick of air-conditioning and commercials on the radio. I was sick of the cell phone. I needed a place where none of those things existed.

I headed cross-country to Sundance, north and down through Upton, Clareton, and other little places that were named by people who were mostly lost, and in being so, managed to define the continent. No radio. No air-conditioning. No phone. No pool. No pets.

I sang "King of the Road" for thirty miles, and it was killer good. It was awesome.

Behind the pickup, a plume of reddish dust rose up and clouded the mirror. The dust smelled real, a musky mix of clay and sand that hung on my arm like my arm hung on the metal frame of the window. I licked my lips, and the taste of the ground dripped off my moustache. I felt connected to this piece of land and slowed down. It occurred to me that people drive slower on roads they know because they have a sense of peace. They taste the ground, and they savor that essence. When you're close to home, you don't need to hurry.

I was far from home, but the air was crisp and honest. I slowed down, and the dust plume followed a breeze to the east. My mirror became as clear as the windshield, and the sun chased the curve of the earth, seeking the source of the wind. I crossed Walker Creek, and somewhere around Lightning Creek, I caught a road headed northeast, and followed it toward the Cheyenne River. Suddenly it was cooler, almost cold. The landscape changed. A sea of sagebrush became an immense labyrinth of draws, gullies, knobs, ridges, and hidey-holes that burst with life.

A band of antelope stood in the departing light, tan-and-white hides gleaming as neon. They watched me approach, then blasted off into the fading light, tiny clouds of dust rising from each hoof, until they were obscured by the dust they made. Around a corner a convention of sharp-tailed grouse clustered on the road, pecking gravel. In a gully to the west, a mule deer buck worked the last of his velvet from an impressive set of antlers.

The temperature plummeted, and I worked my way across a flat stretch of land as lonesome and incredible as any I had ever seen. The Cheyenne River was ahead. The tops of cottonwoods teased me, and in the waning light, tried to make me believe they were sumac or something else. If Lewis and Clark had bought the disguise, they would have gone the other direction and died. I wasn't buying, but I stopped in the midst of nothing, and let the dust settle.

A bunch of black cows milled around the flat. Night-hawks started their strange, whoop-oop-oop hunt for bugs, and somewhere near, a red-tailed hawk offered its last screech of the day. Stars poked their heads out of the night sky, and the moon crept over the Black Hills, iridescent and huge.

The Cheyenne was a trickle of water at best. Mostly, it was a river of grass, an underground seep that ran for hundreds of miles through the Powder River country, on into South Dakota, and then Nebraska, and finally, into the Missouri. The grass along the river bottom was green, but the leaves on the cottonwoods were turning to gold. The trees were evidence of the last big flood, a concurrence of events that led to a mess of mud flats and water that make cottonwoods. By the size of them, I guessed the last flood must have been thirty years ago or more.

I got out and stood on the bridge, which was newer than the trees. From the trees came a gentle tapping, and I strained my eyes to find a flicker, wings orange underneath, stilted flight pattern making him look like he was darting up and down. A little band of turkeys made their way to the river, and in the distance, a cow bawled for her calf.

Across the river, I ran into the first and only human I would see in seventy miles or more.

She was a young girl, probably sixteen or seventeen, and she was out on the sagebrush flat, mounted on a big bay horse. She had light brown hair, pulled in a ponytail and jammed through the flap on the back of a Thar's Feed cap. Her face was tan, with freckles across her nose and cheeks. She was slender and sat the horse like she'd been born there. On any other day, I imagined her teeth would shine when she smiled.

Right now, there was no hint of a smile. I could see the ranch about a half mile to the northwest, and I figured she'd been out there for at least an hour or more.

The picture played out pretty clearly. She had been sent out to get the milk cow, a little Jersey wasp that had taken to the hills. When the cow decided not to cooperate and be driven home, the girl had gotten mad, roped the damn cow, dallied up, and brought her along against her will.

It all worked fine until they got to the gate.

Inside the gate, the horses were as anxious to head for the hills as the milk cow had been. If the girl left the gate open, the horses would leave as the cow arrived, and she would be back out on the flat chasing ponies. Every time she got off to open the gate, the Jersey took it as a sign of weakness and decided to head back south onto the flat. She couldn't hold the cow, even a little Jersey bitch, without a dally around the horn, and she couldn't open the gate from the back of her horse. If she lost the rope, she lost the cow.

One thing was certain. She was not about to go home and ask for help.

I had calculated these options myself a time or two. Tie hard and fast and hope the cow didn't drag the horse away—jump off and open the gate, then jump on and drag her dumb Jersey ass through and close the gate. Or, maybe, pull up a lot of slack and jump off, tie the cow to a post, open the gate and run her sorry butt into the pasture, lead the horse through and close the gate. Other thoughts ran toward getting a gun and shooting the cow or dragging the cow onto the road in front of a speeding truck, but I was the only truck, and I was driving about eight miles an hour.

The look on the girl's face and the lather on the horse indicated maybe she had thought of all these things and more. She was about 100 yards from the gate when I pulled over.

The young lady gathered her reins and her rope and kept one eye on the Jersey and the other one on me.

"I'll get the gate," I hollered, and I pulled the loop and tossed the wire gate to the side.

I was right about the teeth. She grinned, gigged the horse, and took the Jersey through on a trot.

"Thanks a lot!" she yelled, and I grabbed the gate.

"I take it you'd be Neil and Timmy's daughter?" I asked, and she nodded.

"Tell 'em I said hello," I said, and I slid the loop over the gate stick.

I never told the girl my name. She never told me hers.

Three months later, at a meeting in Douglas, Neil and Timmy both thanked me for helping their daughter get the milk cow in. Timmy gave me hell for not coming by for dinner. Neil said they sold the damn milk cow, and nobody missed her a bit.

This is the most special thing about the country, about places where you can see so far that it becomes intimidating. This is the essence of the rural world. Even in the most remote places, the people you meet will be people you know. If not, you strive to find a connection, a common friend, a bond. You look for these things because they always exist. These are the things that make you whole.

I'll get the gate.

FORGIVENESS

I believe in God, but I don't worry too much if God is actually an apparition of Charlton Heston or Alanis Morissette.
I believe Jesus Christ lived, and would have been a very good
director of the US Fish and Wildlife Service, given his ability to
produce lots of fish when none were available. I believe science
and ecology can explain many things in hindsight, but they will
never explain it all. For that, you have to have faith.

I was raised in a family that attended church regularly,
though I have not done the same recently. I was an acolyte, a
member of a youth group, and briefly flirted with conversion to
Catholicism in the interests of a marriage that thankfully never
happened. My most memorable moment in a church, other
than being married to my wife, the baptisms of my three children, and some very moving funerals, was holding hands with
Amy Erickson at a Halloween party in Trinity Episcopal Church
in Lander.

She was dressed as a black cat. I was disguised as a
four-foot-ten gangster, with homemade spats on my shoes. I
was fifteen and she was a year younger. I became fully developed at the age of twenty-three, but she was fully developed
in the eighth grade. That party at the church was a revelation

of sorts, but it was not religious. As things often turn out, we both moved to Casper later in life. She'd outgrown me in many ways, but I lusted for her despite the Ten Commandments. I once thought that Moses should have added an eleventh order, the "Thou shalt not think of Amy Erickson constantly" commandment.

I am a person who prays at odd times. Mostly, I find myself in contemplation when I am happy. Seated on a good horse, with a gentle rain in my face, I find myself thinking more about my spiritual being than my place in time, and in those times I find great peace, and great inspiration. I find spirituality in the smell of sagebrush, blood, animal hair, clean children, and mown hay. I feel the power of God in the sound of thunder, bugling elk, calves bawling for their mothers, rivers, and beavers slapping tails on water. There is peace in the midst of a hurricane of snow, and in the aftermath of white. And, most of all for me, there is a sense of contentment when I traverse this incredible state and see the land as it has evolved for centuries, spreading out in front of us for more miles than most people drive in a decade.

I take pictures of Wyoming. Few publishers are interested. I am told there are no focal points in my photos. They're just grass and sagebrush and sky.

Dumbasses! That's the point. This one is at Manville. The other one is at Carter. And this one, north of Kemmerer, is utterly spectacular. You are looking at a space the size of Rhode Island in the photo, and you can't even see the sheep wagons, or the cows, or the elk, deer, antelope, sage grouse, songbirds, lizards, ponds, frogs, creeks, aspen groves, or the people who live there. This is the real surface of the earth, and it is still there.

I drive over the "Gangplank," that sloping mixture of ancient granite and grass that drop you west to east into Cheyenne and tell my kids about it every time. I tell them this feature is the one John McPhee describes in *Rising from the Plains.*

"At this place, as nowhere else, you can step off the Great Plains directly onto a Rocky Mountain summit."

"We know," the kids say, and they ask me to tell them the story again.

God lives in these places, and so do we.

We have a lot to think about in Wyoming. Everything we value comes from the land around us. When we decide to leave this place, we have to give up some of our values. We leave some part of our soul in Wyoming, because we can't find it anywhere else on the planet.

"God Bless Wyoming and Keep It Wild." So wrote fifteen-year-old Helen Mettler, the last entry in her diary in 1925, and that single statement captured the heart of more than those of us who live here. It is that sentiment that brings people back to the plains, and to the mountains, to a land where the sun sets alone almost every night.

If there is one trait we must adopt and perfect to bless this land and keep it wild, it will be our ability to find forgiveness and acceptance for other points of view. It seems at times as if every choice carries a challenge. Some cynics will tell you if you want to find oil, look for sage grouse; others would say if you want to find sportsmen, look for oil. We ask too much of our landscape sometimes, and we demand too much of our people. Instead of seeking balance, we seem to demand dominance. Have we forgotten how to walk a mile in the other person's shoes?

On Tuesday, a group of Wyoming citizens delivered to the governor a final list of recommendations to help conserve sage grouse. They weren't tossing soft balls. A group of people who represented oil and gas, ranching, conservation, government agencies, and other interests delivered some very direct recommendations. I was honored to work with this group and found the key to the process to be the understanding that we were not intent on stopping anything. Instead, the group looked for ways to manage a situation that could be divisive and devastating to our state.

The discussions were fascinating. Within areas of importance to sage grouse, are there ways we can still develop existing energy resources? It is likely that we can if we get the homework right the first time. Are there places where we will need to preclude development? Of course there are. But, if we operate in an atmosphere of gamesmanship, in a manner best suited to the football field, we will never find those areas of commonality. If we choose to win at all costs, we will either win or we will lose, but either way, at all costs.

Forgiveness leads to optimism, and in the face of countless stories of gloom and doom, I remain an optimist. I truly believe we are smart enough, and passionate enough, to find ways to do things the right way. But, those results will have to come from local initiative and pluck. And in order to maintain optimism, we must engage in a dialogue of understanding, an atmosphere of forgiveness.

I have 50,000 miles on a pickup that is eighteen months old. This week, I have been from Lander to Cheyenne to Sundance and back. I try to schedule driving time at sundown, to see the landscape in its most flattering light. The skin of Wyoming comes alive, and in a culvert near LaGrange sits a swift fox. A herd of elk cross the highway west of Lusk, and red-tailed hawks line the fence posts outside Edgerton. My favorite ranch setting is tucked into a pocket of rolling hills near there. We have challenges, but we have a landscape that largely still holds the natural values it has maintained for centuries. I feel the pressure, but at the same time, I see opportunity.

It is paradoxical that we sometimes insist that nature do all the forgiving, that streams and waterways carry the burden of recovery, that sagebrush must somehow respond to drought, overuse, and removal, that fire be held at bay. Landscapes may forgive, in the sense of recovery, and they may not. When we see the response of plants and animals, whether to rain, management, or other factors, we rejoice.

When we find it in our own nature to be equally forgiving of one another, we should expect the same.

I believe our faith drives our ability to forgive, and to think optimistically. In the book *The Real All Americans* by Sally Jenkins, Harriet Beecher Stowe described the sound of Kiowa prayer as "particularly mournful. It was what the Bible so often speaks of in relation to prayer, a cry unto God."

This is particularly confounding, because in my own experience and relation to the Great Spirit, prayers have been hopeful, a call for guidance, peace, humor, and integrity. It is in that atmosphere of contemplation and hope that miracles take place on our landscape, and the success stories are many.

Near Lake DeSmet, a handful of landowners, conservationists, and habitat managers decided to pool their resources and manage for livestock, wildlife, and the future. Now, more than forty ranchers are engaged in habitat improvements for sage grouse. We see the same dedication in the Shirley Basin, in the Thunder Basin, on rivers and streams in Niobrara and Carbon Counties. Farmers in Goshen County are in the process of converting more than 250 acres of fields and pastures to wetlands, a gesture to migrating waterfowl, shorebirds, wading birds, and countless species of songbirds that will nest in those habitats.

The partnerships and the progress move forward at an unparalleled pace. We need to recognize that those things only happen when we find in ourselves the capacity to respect one another. We should truly "seek to understand, not to be understood." The friendships we make may live beyond the grasses we plant, the rivers we restore, or the aspens we help to sprout.

SANCTUARY

It was a perfect day.

Bald Mountain was hidden in a porridge of snow and fog, and the rim of the canyon was a mere shadow to the north. A thick rime of hoarfrost clung to every plant, rendering their brittleness silent. Wheat grasses stood frozen like carved ivory chopsticks; willows muted from crimson to pink in the early light. The white bark of bare aspens disappeared in the mist, and giant firs created an ominous, shadowy backdrop to nothingness.

Snow fell straight down, light and fluffy, each flake catching the morning sun like a tiny prism, scattering a kaleidoscope across the valley. Moisture sank into the leaves of sage, pine, and sand, creating a musky cologne. Not far below me, a bull elk whistled a bored, late-season bugle; cows and calves barked and mewed at one another, and silence reigned again.

I sat on a sandstone ridge, just below the skyline, scanning the floodplain below. As the sun rose higher, ambers, olives, and magentas of plant life lost their disguise. Coyote willow along the creek, and in the margins of old streams. Yellow willow scattered in clumps. Sage and rabbitbrush clustered between the lowlands. Once-green meadows now golden, undulating through the mélange of color and diversity. Between the cold air, snow, fog, and early light, I found myself in a pastel watershed where nothing was clear.

A chickadee changed all that.

Oblivious to all of the sensory stimuli around, the tiny black-and-white ball of fluff popped onto a branch of a limber pine and bounced snow down the back of my neck. That much done, the bird hopped to another branch and did it again. I found the bird no more than five feet away, and my dissolved world of abstract color was suddenly one of intense detail. At close range, the tiny yellow flanks of the chickadee became feathers, one layered atop the other. Sleek black head. Shiny eyes. The bird cocked its head, looked me over, and darted to another perch.

The chickadee weighed less than my wedding ring, and nearly every moment of its existence was dependent on finding enough food to fuel a metabolism that darted and danced on a permanent basis. It was perched in a tree that measured success in rings the size of a chickadee's toe, an ancient relic content to extract moisture from fog, the ability to take moisture from rain, snow, sleet, or dew. In hard times, the tree could shut itself off from the world and do little or nothing.

Survivors, both.

I knew I would not see an elk in the meadows below me. I had known that when I sat under the crest of the ridge, below the pine tree, with the smell of wet sand and sage beneath my ass. It was part of the deal, hunting elk where the advantage was all theirs, where they knew every inch of the landscape, and I knew less. It was part of the yearning, the excitement. Mostly, it was a prelude to ritual that was more than religion or rite. If I wanted to find an elk, I would have to go where they were safe, into their world. I relished the hike, and whether I found or killed an elk, deer, moose, or any living thing, this place was my favorite place on earth.

I started down the sandy hill, boots sinking into sugar-soft colluvium that would soon find its way to the creek, every step intent on avoiding crunchy snow left over from the last storm. At the bottom, I found a place to cross the creek, skirting the ice, trying to be as quiet as possible, knowing every wild creature within miles could hear me coming. It occurred to me that maybe it was I who didn't want to hear the noise of my clumsiness, and in my mind, I became invisible and silent. I crossed the barbed wire fence and started across the meadow. The only sound was the steady, rambunctious rattle of water beginning a long trip to the Pacific Ocean.

It was a half mile across the meadow, and my step felt light, nearly silent. Out in the open, the snow swirled harder; a mean wind blasted off the mountains and burned the skin. I was leaning into the face of the storm hard enough that if the wind should stop, I might fall over. When the pain was intolerable, I turned around and looked back at the long ridge the wind skipped over like a stone on water. On top of that ridge, the storm was omnipresent. Six feet below the crest, I remembered a chickadee bobbing up and down on a pine bough, completely out of the wind. I had walked less than a mile, and the world around me had changed measurably more than twice. In the middle of the meadow, I could see sanctuary behind, and sanctuary ahead, but my immediate world was nothing but hell.

From the outside, the Fredell Place was nothing special, another ranch, another broken dream. Homesteaded in the late 1890s, bound tight by cold and distance, the place was for sale within twenty years. My grandfather tried to buy the place from his uncle in the 1920s and was turned away. The uncle refused to carry the note, and the deal never happened. A young man with passion was stopped in his tracks, and a ranch of dreams became a reality of naught. Life went on.

Now, some sixty years later, the place was largely unchanged. The road in was wider, but it still blew shut in winter. The ditches in the meadows were cleaned with a single pass of a tractor and ditcher, instead of a horse and slip, but the water came from the same headgate, and ran across the same terrain. The old cabin had been replaced with a modest, modern house, but the view was the same. A few oil wells and a pipeline were newer, but only since the 1950s. But this land was still owned by the same family, now a generation removed, despite some really hard times.

A fence of wooden posts and rusted wires divided the meadow from the bog. I could see the posts in the fog and snow, but I could feel the transition better at my feet. Between bog and meadow there coursed an arterial channel of water that defined the boundary between wilderness and agrarian desire. Beneath

my boots the line was fuzzy, but at my shins, the height and thick-
ness of vegetation was telltale. It was a matter of feet at the most,
but there were scars in the meadow, lines where teams of horses
and machines crossed the line and found themselves mired in the
world of the swamp, suddenly ground to a halt by the desire to
gain just one more bite of grass.

I stopped and looked at my boots. The tops were dry.
Water came from beneath the soles and found level between my
feet and the land, about a quarter inch above my footprint. From
here on, geologic time and natural process were reality. I was
merely one participant in a snowstorm, in a perfect place, at a
perfect time.

Bits of hoarfrost hung on the barbs of the fence, and the
only evidence of my passage was two stretches of now bare wire
where my hands had held it down. Here, the willows were taller,
another species better suited to the bog. This willow grew in
huge clumps, with a root mass as great as the twisted canopy
above my head, and between the willows ran a labyrinth of
trails and passages, each suited to the scat beneath the branches.
Wider trails were dominated by moose and elk manure. Those
most dense offered only a memento of rabbit droppings and
mouse tracks.

As many times as I had walked into this place, every entry
inside the bog seemed new and different. There were really only a
handful of passages from the meadow into the woods. Fifty yards
into the willows I saw my own track from a week before and
smiled. Creature of habit. All water eventually finds the bottom of

the hill. There was little difference between me and the creatures I sought. Now, it was a matter of how well each of us knew the ground beneath our feet, luck, and timing.

The willow thicket gave way to a deep sea of tall sedges and a steaming stream of thermal water that defined the south edge of the woodlands. Snow streamed down. Fog steamed up. The whole place was an ethereal wilderness of muted color and sound. The water itself was a strange bluish color, unique to geo-thermal springs, and on the edges of the creek grew pastel lichens and other plants that could stand the extremes in temperature. On the other side of the stream, very little grew at all. Massive firs occupied the high spots, their roots gnarled and twisted like the legs of so many collided dancers. Beneath the ancient fir trees, an ashen-gray muck oozed into the low ground.

This aquamarine stream mesmerized me. I had chased it upstream to its genesis, a measly trickle of water that surged from beneath a rock. I followed the channel to its terminus, a wide swamp where water seemed to wear thin and vanish. Four miles downstream, the same pastel colors and eerie soils popped up in a vast wetland local folks called the "soap holes." The lower bog was easy enough to find; eight huge firs stood sentinel on the high spots. Between the two, the geology was simpler. Sand and rock. Ancient streambeds. Glacial till.

A red squirrel chattered out a shrill warning to some-thing or someone and brought me back to the here and now. I always thought squirrels were saved from extinction by their lack of flesh; maybe it was the incessant noise that deterred sensible predators. It was simply not possible for *everything* to be a threat to the forest, as squirrels seemed to constantly insist.

I crossed the warm stream and found myself in yet another world. Snow barely made it through the boughs of fir; sunlight rarely found the earth. An old hewn stump betrayed the removal of one fir, long ago. Charred remains of another fir told the story of another harvest. This was a place where the actions of man and nature were separated by centuries, evident now, and essentially the same.

A wide trail snaked through the timber, tracks going in both directions. Moose, elk, deer, bear, and mountain lion prints were jumbled into a semifrozen quilt of mud. Elk tracks were on top, edges still soft. To the east, a cow elk squeaked at her calf, and the call was returned. I moved to the north, out of the forest, into an ancient amalgamation of beaver dams, now filled with silt and vegetation. The dams were barely evident, a few sticks here and there, each decadent pond lined with a wall of willows on the downstream side. Some still held shallow pools of water. Most were filled with grass.

Between the long-forgotten streambed and the current, a slender island of sage and rabbitbrush bisected the willows. A small bunch of mule deer browsed absently, then began to lie down for the day. A magpie landed on a tall sagebrush and launched into a cacophonous attempt to rival the squirrel. Within moments, there were half a dozen squawking birds, and I used their cover to sneak downstream.

The elk were right where I expected them to be, lying behind a patch of willows, no more than fifty yards away. Snow was piling up in front of them, but the willows kept them dry.

Their heads were in the air, knowing I was there, wondering where. A big, dark cow stood up and shook her head, turned around, and lay down. Farther from the cows and calves, a big bull hunkered under an old willow.

I put the rifle stock to my cheek and stared down the barrel. Clean, easy shot. I could feel my moustache turning to ice. Water dripped from my hat down my neck. Meat in the pan.

I walked out of the bog as quietly as I had walked in. Found a new place to cross the warm spring. Threw a rock at the obnoxious squirrel. Missed. Felt the wind at my back as I crossed the meadow.

This storm would be a good one. There was a good six inches of wet snow on the meadow now, and the sky was dark and low. The air was still, and moisture came straight down, in gigantic flakes. Even the sandy ridge was wet now, and my breath came shorter as I climbed back to the top.

I stared back at the place I had been and smiled. In all the years I had hunted there, I had never once fired a shot. I had a thousand reasons—the willows were in the way—it was too hard to get the carcass out—I couldn't get a clear shot— they spooked—they weren't there. Even when I told myself it was my respect for my prey, I knew I was lying. This was *my* place of sanctuary.

EPILOGUE

"**A**ll things are connected. Whatever befalls the earth befalls the children of the earth."

Those words are attributed to Chief Seattle of the Suquamish and Duwamish tribes, but they might be the words of many who work in the natural world. When I began my career, every single issue was a battle to be won or lost, a chance for immortality or ignominy. No holds barred. Winner take all.

It never worked that way, even though we rallied with our supporters and insisted it was so. Usually, we all lost, and in losing, we lost sight of the most important thing of all.

Conservation is not about science or politics. It is not about laws and restrictions and winning and losing. It doesn't "just happen." No—conservation is a combination of ecology, economy, and culture, a blend of all three that requires an intricate balance.

Unfortunately, balance is not an average, though it is often portrayed as such. Balance is the intricate beauty that allows a butterfly to feed on a flower and pollinate other flowers to feed other butterflies, but it has to include the cow that mows down the grass so the flowers might bloom and allow the flowers to open so the butterflies might feed. Balance comes when the whole is more important that the minutiae—when the details fill the holes.

Ultimately, conservation is about people, and people can be very difficult. While we actually agree on many, many things, we tend to malinger and obsess on our differences. We comprehend science, yet pick and choose which science to follow. We argue the price of beef instead of the value of the cow as a meadow manager.

Thankfully, science, economics, and politics aside, few of us are not moved by the first flight of a yellow warbler, the croaking of frogs, or the wobbling first steps of a newborn calf. We are drawn to life—to water, to new leaves on the trees, to wind and cold and penetrating heat, and each other. Like horses, we don't want to be separated from the bunch, even if we get kicked or bitten once in a while. And, like horses, sometimes we work best when we are away from the bunch and able to concentrate on the steer in our headlights.

Somewhere in my journey, I found that if I would look for things I had in common with others, they would become the most important things, and oddly, the easiest to achieve. It might be something as simple as a song, a poem, a bird, or often, another human being. Within each of us there is a connection to every person we meet. When we seek that commonality, we will find not only incredible opportunity, but a sense of peace, and a sense of place. We will find that all things are connected, and most of all we will find connections that propel us forward. If we want to achieve conservation, it will come from our ability to work together and heed the adage that "sometimes God calms the storm—sometimes God calms the child and lets the storm rage."

We live in an irrational world. We desire simplicity and crave complexity. We ask for privacy, yet relish gossip. At the same time we demand perfection, we seek absolution for our own faults. We are fiercely competitive, independent, and driven. We have progressed from horse-drawn machinery to rocketry, pencil to smartphone, sextant to satellite. We can put more information than the human brain can contain into something smaller than the trimmings from our fingernails. We are omnipotent, at the apex of our knowledge.

Maybe. Maybe not.

We do quite well with things we control. When it comes to chemistry, physics, and math, we are incredible. We can build structures, precision automobiles, spaceships, and computers. Our capacity to apply technology is something else indeed.

But when we face fire, flood, or other natural phenomena, we are lost in the woods. And when we try to command respect from the natural world, we are almost uniformly rebuked. Like a long-spurned lover, natural process can be a seething stalker, focused, obsessive, and very, very patient.

I was taught that Benjamin Franklin coined the adage, "Constant dropping wears away stones." It was a short little phrase that meant a lot to me in many ways, one of those things you carry around in your head and find handy when you expect it least.

In reality, the reference is much, much older. Chaucer used a similar line in *The Canterbury Tales* in the late four-teenth century, and the Book of Job says simply that "water wears away stones."

In the sixth century BCE Lao Tzu wrote, "Water is fluid, soft, and yielding. But water will wear away rock, which is rigid and cannot yield. As a rule, whatever is fluid, soft, and yielding will overcome whatever is rigid and hard. This is another paradox: "what is soft is strong."

Oddly enough, to escape the order and precision and demands of our "real worlds," we seek absolution and order from a world where order is built upon chaos and chance. While our personal worlds absorb more complexity, we demand that natural systems conform to our arrogant sense of order.

The natural world is a paradox, fluid and powerful, alive with and without air, patient enough to wait for the next shift in tectonic plates, eruption of the volcano, lightning to ignite the fire. We are not meant to understand every nuance of this world. We can only track what happens, and hope that we are patient enough to do those things that will allow chaos and chance to maintain an elegant mess that goes far beyond our own selfish lifetimes.

We have to rethink the way we connect to the natural world, to become soft and strong, to allow the patience of nature to find its way into ourselves, and not the other way around. This book has taken too long to write because it is an ongoing story of my own quest for calm in the storm. I learned long ago that I cannot control nature.

All I can do is listen, learn, and share what I see. Through rain and snow, warm summer days, life and death, I may have learned a few things. Beyond that, my only role in the natural world is to place my trust in the next generation of those who really care enough to let the world work, and I am completely good with that.

ACKNOWLEDGMENTS

There is no way to thank all of the people who have made this book a reality by name, so I will not try to do so. I have been blessed to live in a world where I was not judged, but welcomed by others who shared my passion, gave me vision, picked me up when I was down, and knocked me down when I was a jackass. Looking back, at every step of my life, some other human emerged to make me better, and that is a very humbling realization.

I was lucky enough to be born into a family of pranksters and hard workers, a clan that disregarded how many "steps removed" we might be from one another—we were just family. Thank you all for being my brothers and sisters, aunts and uncles, surrogate moms and dads, and mostly for being my friends.

Chief among the pranksters and hard workers are my parents, Bill and Carrie, who allowed me to roam far from home and always come back. Dad, you gave me an incredible view of the natural world. Mom, thank you for making sure I understood history, culture, and the arts. Together you taught me about the most important things in life—integrity, honor, respect, curiosity, passion, and loyalty.

I have been fortunate in my life to live the adage that "when the pupil is ready, the teacher will emerge," so to all of my mentors, and there are hundreds, thank you for your patience and your wisdom. You live within me. I find you often in my thoughts, and that brings me both peace and humor.

I owe a special debt to Rick and Heather Knight, who insisted that I finish this book, and went above and beyond to help make it happen. You truly are the "radical center" and an inspiration always.

I cannot say enough about the crew at Fulcrum. Patty Maher and Bob Baron were my initial contacts, and they were so welcoming and encouraging that this book became a complete joy to write. Every step of the way, this was an endeavor of passion, and Kateri Kramer, Alison Auch, and Sam Scinta were there at every turn. I am a better person for meeting them.

Thanks to my children, Joe, Jake, and Maggie for giving me inspiration and insight, hope, and sometimes, too much anxiety. You made me a better man, and continue to do that every day.

Finally, I must acknowledge my incredible wife, Lynn, who has labored through every version of every essay, taken the wrath of a frustrated writer, and stood her ground to make the words in this book right, and better. Every step of this journey would have been impossible without her.

ABOUT THE AUTHOR

Bob Budd is a fifth-generation Wyoming native and has worked throughout the West on natural resource issues for more than forty years. He has a master of science degree in range management and bachelor of science degrees in agricultural business and animal science from the University of Wyoming. He has worked as executive director of the Wyoming Stock Growers Association, managed ranches and other lands for The Nature Conservancy, and is currently the executive director of the Wyoming Wildlife and Natural Resource Trust, a state agency dedicated to maintaining and restoring natural landscapes and ecological function in Wyoming. He is a past president of the International Society for Range Management and the Wyoming chapter of The Wildlife Society, and a past public relations chairman for Cheyenne Frontier Days. He has facilitated management plans for the Big Sandy River, bighorn sheep, and most recently, sage grouse in Wyoming and the West. Bob and his wife, Lynn, live in Cheyenne and have three grown children, Joe, Jake, and Maggie.